REMEMBERING THE PAST
SHAPING THE FUTURE

REMEMBERING THE PAST
SHAPING THE FUTURE

GERMANY CLOSE UP

HENTRICH & HENTRICH

Content

Foreword from the German Federal Ministry of Economics and Technology

Ernst Burgbacher, Parliamentary State Secretary of the Federal Ministry of Economics and Technology, Former Member of Parliament (1998–2013)

Dear Friends and Alumni of *Germany Close Up – American Jews Meet Modern Germany*, Dear Ladies and Gentlemen,

Through encounters with other people we create a basis for mutual understanding. This mutual understanding is essential for the development of any friendship – something which is not only true for friendships between two individuals, but also for those between nations. This realization was a major impulse behind the initiation of the youth encounter program Germany Close Up. This program enables young, Jewish North Americans to visit Germany for one to two weeks. Many participants come holding an image of Germany that is particularly associated with the years between 1933 and 1945. Often, they are from families, which suffered greatly under the atrocities that were committed during this time. These memories continue to impact on the younger generation of these families today.

Germany Close Up offers its young participants an intensive educational and cultural program made up of personal exchanges, encounters, and visits. The program itinerary provides them with the opportunity to learn about Germany's history in the field, and to form their own opinions and create their own picture of Germany and German-Jewish life. At the same time, they meet young Germans of the same age and participate in discussions with politicians and creative professionals. The insights gained by participants during their trip are further enriched by visits to museums and memorial sites.

In the following essays, former participants describe in a haunting and moving way how their visit not only influenced their image of Germany, but also how it has affected the way in which they perceive themselves. Participants are filled with conflicting feelings when they come to our country. Often, these feelings deeply affect the personalities of these young people. Their reports offer a striking illustration of the reflections triggered by their visit to Germany and how these experiences can lead to the creation of new opinions and attitudes.

It is, however, not only the participants themselves who benefit from the personal encounters they have here in Germany. The reports show an outsiders view of Germany, which stimulate and sensitize their German counterparts to different ways of seeing and understanding German-American and German-Jewish relations. A good relationship is not something to be taken for granted and requires constant nurturing through communicative exchange. This fact is something that emerges very clearly from these essays.

I am pleased that through the Germany Close Up program, the Federal Government is making an important contribution towards fostering exchange and, ultimately, understanding between Jewish North Americans and Germans. This is in keeping with the spirit of the former Foreign Secretary of the United States, George Marshall, who, luckily, prevailed with his idea for the reconstruction of war damaged Europe. He was the *spiritus rector* of the European Recovery Program, which provides the context in which the Germany Close Up program operates today. Reconstruction and financial investment following the end of the war served to build up the economic links, which still act as the basis for unifying friendships and partnerships today. George Marshall was consequently awarded the Nobel Peace Prize for his efforts to rebuild war ravaged Europe.

The European Reconstruction Program of North America continues to live on today in Germany in the form of the ERP Special Fund. Out of the North American Reconstruction Program for Europe has grown a transatlantic friendship between nations that is firmly rooted in history. This friendship is anchored in freedom, democracy, and justice. Germany Close Up is also born of this same spirit, and is an expression of Germany's gratitude to the North American people for their friendship and support over the past several decades.

This publication, comprising the reports of Germany Close Up participants, not only documents the experiences of the young people involved. It also stirs the reader's interest to embrace an intensive and open exchange between the two countries, and through this, aims to help develop a better mutual understanding and to challenge personal attitudes and adopted opinions. I wish all future participants of this program similarly interesting and moving personal experiences in Germany as those documented in this publication. I wish all who read these essays valuable food for thought, and that these reports may perhaps even serve as a source of inspiration for finding new ways of sustaining and strengthening the current positive transatlantic, German-Jewish relationship into the future.

Best regards,
Ernst Burgbacher

Foreword from the German Federal Foreign Office

Harald Leibrecht, Coordinator of Transatlantic Cooperation in the Federal Foreign Office, Former Member of Parliament (2002–2013)

Dear Friends and Alumni of *Germany Close Up – American Jews Meet Modern Germany*, Dear Ladies and Gentlemen,

In 2012, less than five years after being established, *Germany Close Up* celebrated its 1000th participant. I have met only a few of the participating young Jews from the U.S. and Canada personally, but every single encounter made an impression on me. I was impressed by the participants' accounts of the personal stories that brought them to Berlin and of the family discussions held prior to their traveling to the "country of the Shoah." Yet, I was even more impressed by the attentive and intelligent observations that they made during their stay in Germany and by their ability to reflect on these observations both within their group and with their German interlocutors.

The essays published in this book are the best examples of this. Past and present, guilt and reconciliation, concentration camps and memorials, but also galleries and clubs, discussions on green energy and European integration, climate change and foreign policy and, of course, Jewish life in modern Germany make the *Germany Close Up* experience challenging, intense, diverse, and unique at the same time. The essays provide a special impression of the personal experiences of some of the American and Canadian participants during their brief stay in Germany.

For the Federal Foreign Office, *Germany Close Up* is the flagship program of German-American-Jewish dialogue. I am pleased that so many Jewish American students and young professionals choose to visit Germany and meet with Germans from all walks of life. The wide spectrum of organizations, institutions, and individuals that have cooperated with *Germany Close Up* is the best proof of the program's success.

I wish *Germany Close Up* all the best for the future and hope that its alumni community will continue to thrive.

With best regards,
Harald Leibrecht

Germany Close Up participants on a walking tour of Jewish Berlin Mitte

Germany Close Up participants lighting candles at a commemoration ceremony for Kristallnacht in Berlin

Editors' Preface

Dagmar Pruin, Director,
Germany Close Up,
Aktion Sühnezeichen Friedensdienste e.V.

Hermann Simon, Director,
New Synagogue Berlin – Centrum Judaicum Foundation

When we received the mandate to initiate *Germany Close Up – American Jews Meet Modern Germany* five years ago, we could hardly have imagined the journey that this program would end up taking us on. Since our first trip in the Fall of 2007, more than 1400 young, North American Jews have visited Germany through our program. During this time, we have shared very different days and experiences with our participants: days that made us cry and days that made us laugh; days full of dark memories and days full of sparkling hope for the future.

In 2009 and again in 2011, we asked our program alumni to share some of their memories and reflections on these days and experiences with us. We did this in the form of two essay competitions. After reading through all of the essays entered into these two competitions, we were so moved by many of the contributions that we found it sad to think that besides ourselves, no one else may ever read these. Out of this feeling emerged the idea to put together a small collection of some of these essays in order to share the memories and reflections they contain with a wider public. The resulting collection is contained in the book you are now holding.

The essays, the thoughts they share, and the forms they take, are as various as the authors themselves. In a reflection of the diverse range of participants we have had on our programs, the authors of the essays collected in this volume all come from diverse religious and political backgrounds and from families with very different histories and life experiences. Together, all of these factors color the impressions and reflections of the authors in many different ways.

The starting point for many of the essays collected here is the Shoah. Indeed, the shadow of the Shoah is something that all of our programs must answer to. Against this backdrop, all those involved with Germany Close Up continually find themselves confronted by enormous emotional challenges. Not only program participants, but also the Germans they encounter are continually called to question and confront issues related to both Germany's past and present. Indeed, the itineraries of the Germany Close Up trips are designed to encourage and enable discussion of these issues, by presenting participants with different perspectives and narratives on both.

Neue Synagoge, Berlin

In taking the Shoah as their starting point, the following essays show some of the various attempts made by participants to come to terms with and express the often conflicting feelings it arouses. Although each participant has their own way of dealing with this, two main lines of expression are evident in these essays. Many of the authors trace a line of continuity from the past to the present. In other essays, however, there is a palpable break in the text, symbolic of the break that the extermination of the Jews of Europe still presents today.

Moving on from this starting point, the essays also reflect on the different topics raised during our programs: history and memory; remembrance and memorialization; loss and hope; identity and religion; perception and layers of meaning. An underlying tenor running through all of the essays is the simultaneous need to remember the sadness of the past while also looking positively towards the future. For many, this is a future, which can be actively shaped through meaningful dialogue. This common, underlying tenor is reflected in the title we have chosen for the collection "Remembering the past – Shaping the future."

In addition to reflecting on the topics raised during the program, the following essays also process the experiences that the authors had during their time in Germany. At the core of all Germany Close Up programs stand the encounters that participants have. These encounters may be with different places, such as memorials, buildings, streets, or empty spaces, and their history. Perhaps more significantly, however, these encounters may be with people. The essays in this volume share with the reader the impressions that these personal encounters and discussions left on the authors. While official encounters with political and societal representatives, such as members of the German Federal Parliament, are valuable for participants, some of the most important encounters are those that participants had with young Germans of a similar age. Equally important are the encounters with the Jewish communities in Germany, which often challenge the perspectives of our participants.

The essays in this collection can be read in any order, on their own or all together. We have, however, given some thought to the order in which they are presented. The collection is parenthesized by the two winning essays: Hadas Cohen's winning essay from 2009 and Louis Mittel's winning essay from 2011. The tones of these two essays stand in stark contrast to one another and place them at opposing ends of the range of feelings expressed by all of the authors in this volume. The remaining essays lie at different points along this line and are ordered to reflect this. The volume begins with those essays, which concentrate on issues related to the past and which pose questions about how this should be remembered and memorialized. The volume then moves on to essays more focused on the time participants spent in Germany on Germany Close Up. Finally, the volume concludes with those essays, which focus more strongly on hope for the future against the backdrop of the past. Whilst this description may give the impression that the essays included in this volume follow a fluid development, this is not the case. Indeed, just as there is sometimes a noticeable break within a single essay, there is occasionally also a noticeable break between one essay and the next.

We would also like to take this opportunity to express our thanks to a number of people. The success of Germany Close Up over the last six years has only been made possible by the support and commitment of our many individual and institutional partners. Our thanks go to our partners in the German Federal Ministry of Economics and Technology and the German Federal Foreign Office for their continued financial and institutional support. We would also like to thank the countless politicians, diplomats, journalists, academics, students, and young adults, who have given up their time to meet with our participants and provide them with the opportunity to encounter everyday Germans. Our thanks also go to the Jewish communities in Germany, as well as the Jewish institutions, both in Germany and North America, who help make our program possible. In particular, we would like to thank the staff of the Centrum Judaicum and Germany Close Up, who invest so much of their time and energy into realizing the program. Most especially, however, we would like to thank all of our program alumni for participating in Germany Close Up. Ultimately, it is the courage that they show in placing themselves in our hands and opening themselves to the uncertainties and challenges of our trip that make Germany Close Up and the experiences described in this book possible.

We are particularly pleased that this volume has been published by the publishing house Hentrich & Hentrich. Hentrich & Hentrich is a Berlin based publishing house that specializes in publications with a focus on Jewish culture, life, and contemporary history. Its existence is symbolic of the reemergence of Jewish life in Berlin and Germany and the growing public interest in Jewish topics.

Reading through the essays when they were submitted to our two essay competitions, we were struck by the at times heartwarming, at times sorrowful, but always thought provoking insights and impressions of contemporary Germany that our program participants took home with them. It was a pleasure and a privilege to be privy to these often very personal reflections. We hope that you enjoy reading the following essays as much as we have.

Dagmar Pruin and Hermann Simon,
Berlin 2013

The Impossibilities of Transcendence – or why I felt bad because my Grandparents did not have to survive Auschwitz

Hadas Cohen

To articulate my impressions of Germany, I need to start from the beginning, and the beginning is in Israel, where I was born.

Growing up there, I always felt somehow inadequate in comparison to my friends. True, half of my family on my mother's side was killed during the Second World War. Yet, no one survived Auschwitz, or any other famous extermination camp for that matter, and neither of my grandparents had numbers tattooed on their forearms. In fact, whenever us kids in the family asked questions about the past, awkward silences came up, so at some point we stopped asking.

In my mother's family no one ever really talked about these things. What I do remember are a few stories about nine out of my grandfather's thirteen siblings disappearing, their fate unknown, or the murder of my grandmother's youngest sister. These stories, which I heard from my mother, and even she was not exactly sure of the details, seemed like semi-vivid dreams one can hardly remember after waking up. Looking back, I am astounded by how little I understood of the meaning of these silences back then.

In Israel, every April, we commemorate the Holocaust on a special day to remind us of what happened and to ensure that we will never forget. As a child I remember that on that day I was glued to the TV, both attracted and appalled, as I watched the black and white documentaries about the camps. I remember pictures of bodies piled up, and stacks of human hair and shoes taken from the victims before they were sent to the gas chambers. Film footage showing lines of sickly thin naked people waiting to be killed was mixed with heartbreaking testimonies of survivors, along with stories about medical experiments conducted by Dr. Mengele. The absence of history within my own family was compensated by the national one I saw on television. These documentaries filled in the gaps created by my grandparents' silences, for whom, I now realize, no words could articulate what had happened "there."

At the same time, as if in a parallel universe that had nothing to do with the national commemoration of the Holocaust or my family's silences, my parents took my sister and me on a trip to Germany during the summer between fourth and fifth grade. I remember my sister and I fighting endlessly in the back of a rented car as we traveled from France to Belgium, and then finally to Germany. The trip was fun, and the Germans we met had nothing to do with the SS soldiers I saw on TV on Holocaust Day. Back then I was completely unaware that on our road-trip in 1982 we most likely did come across one or two German perpetrators who had managed to evade judgment and who were reabsorbed into German society without having paid for what they had done.

Fast-forward a few decades and I am back in Germany, this time with the Germany Close Up group on a trip I was hesitant to take. Since my Israeli childhood, I have moved to New York City, where I am now pursuing a Ph.D. in Political Science. I am writing my dissertation about the Israeli-Palestinian conflict, and about how the memory of the Holocaust is related to the occupation of the Palestinian people. In New York, I have very good German friends, and I have even been to Berlin once before for a friend's wedding.

I had been hesitant to go on this trip because I was aware of the "Holocaust industry," and I did not want to participate in what I believe to be the confiscation of memory by an agenda that aims at making political gains. At the same time, I knew that Berlin is amazing, and Germany, I remembered from my previous trips, is much more than just the Holocaust. And besides, I was beyond all of that. So when the opportunity presented itself, I decided to go.

Berlin

The trip starts in high spirits. Berlin, one of the most important art capitals of the world, teases us seductively on the first night of our arrival. When aimlessly walking through the city with two other group members, we come across a gallery opening in the Hackesche Höfe. The theme of the show, affordable art, is unfathomable in my New York mindset. Affordable what? Only 200 Euros for a beautiful black and white photograph I can see perfectly placed above my desk? I like this city, I think, and I have to restrain myself from buying the picture. From the gallery opening we continue to a trendy Vietnamese restaurant, where we are surrounded by beautiful people. The city feels like a stylish, more sophisticated, and definitely more socialist New York.

But Berlin is also one big memorial site, and with the group I am taken to see a Jewish Synagogue that was destroyed during Kristallnacht, which comes to life in front of my eyes as if right out of a history book. The cemetery-like memorial monument at the city center is impressive and chilling at the same time. Later, the Jewish Museum with its dark tower evokes in me a suffocating anxiety when the heavy doors of the towers close behind us, and we are locked inside for a long minute.

In hindsight, I notice that the grander the Holocaust memorials, the quicker and more efficiently my emotional defenses spring up to shield me from that horrific past. What was astounding, however, was the way the small things, the ones which surprise you and which you cannot anticipate, manage to penetrate and leave their mark. Those things were not the way Germany dealt with its Nazi past as a nation, but rather the everyday practices adopted and enacted by "regular" Germans. I find out, for example, that certain German words are no longer used because they are considered to be Nazi terminology. I see small brass memory stones implanted in Berlin's sidewalks with the names of dead Nazi victims outside the buildings from which they were taken to their death. Germans who live in these buildings today, I am told, are the ones who initiate and pay for the construction of these stones. No government sponsors this project, nor has it been imposed from above with someone else deciding what to remember and how to feel. No, this is coming from the "bottom up," and it is one of the ways Germans today choose to make sense of their past.

We are taken to see the Parliament and we meet Member of Parliament Hans-Ulrich Klose, who tells us how much Germans love Obama. We listen to classical music, and one night I go out with local friends to a "silent" concert, where the audience is given headphones for a simultaneous individual and group experience. Every night we go out to different cozy restaurants, followed by drinks at candle-lit bars. We dance at a club inside an old factory building, with cathedral-like high ceilings, and old paintings on the walls. In New York, I hardly ever go out to clubs, but here I dance the night away. I cannot get enough of the city, and on the third day of the trip I decide that when I get back to New York I will look for fellowships and move to Kreuzberg! There, in that quaint ethnic neighborhood that young hipsters share with Turkish immigrants, I will write my dissertation.

Yet, Berlin, this hip, artistic city, is a city that similarly to Germany as a whole, exists under the daunting shadow of a complicated past. On one of our daily group tours we walk along the remains of the Wall, with a former East Berliner guide telling us the history of the division of the country after the Second

World War. She shows us a subway map they had back then, on which the graphics are drawn only up to the borders of the former GDR, which ended at the Wall separating East from West Berlin. Beyond that border, as if in a nightmarish distorted reality, the map is white. I can only try to imagine what it must have been like to live under such a regime, which does not allow the existence, even as a mere possibility, of what it cannot tolerate.

The Camp

And then, on the next day, my own private demons are unleashed. On a dreary morning we are taken to Sachsenhausen, a former concentration camp next to the city of Oranienburg, located an hour away from Berlin. I see that some of the houses at the edge of the town face the walls surrounding the camp. From their windows, I think, one had to see what was going on inside. I realize that even those who lived within the town itself, away from the camp, must have seen the shackled prisoners running through the city every day on their way to the slave labor sites. At this point of the tour I am still emotionally intact and removed. "This did not happen to me," I keep on telling myself, "and this is not happening now." We continue with our tour into the campground itself. I am physically cold, and the umbrella cannot shield me from the heavy rain. All I want is to be warm and to go back, yet our guide takes us deeper and deeper into the campground, away from the comfort of the visitors' center. I start to think about the twenty-four hour roll calls those brought here had to endure during rain, shine, or snow, and I see the machine guns poised on top of the watch towers pointed at the prisoners to ensure their obedience.

I am haunted by how it must have felt to be brought here, to a lawless land where the opposite of what we perceive to be humanity set the norm. Where inmates were yelled instructions in a language they could not understand and where disobeying would result in being shot immediately to death. Similarly to my experience when I first watched Leni Riefenstahl's *Triumph of the Will*, I feel as though all of this is directed at me. That if I had been there, I would have been the one dragged away and... And I stop, it is simply too much, I cannot be here anymore, I need to get out. My academic "protective shield" is gone, and the distance between being here now and being here back then melts away. In my mind, the barrier between nightmares and reality no longer exists.

We finally return to the warm bus, which takes us back to Berlin. The trip continues, but I am changed. It is a process I am still undergoing, and which I still try to make sense of. But what I do know is that I saw something there, a chilling side of human nature I know we all possess, a side that is very rarely unleashed. And the most horrific of all, I realize, is that all my degrees and all my education would have meant nothing in there. Now I understand why I did not want to go on this trip, why despite my extensive travels all over the world, I never went to Eastern Europe, the land of the camps. The inescapable reality is this – I am Jewish, and if I had been there back then walking on the very ground I am now walking on as a free woman it would have been me in the nightmarish documentaries I saw as a child on Holocaust Day.

Facing the Demons and Still No Answers

When I came back from the trip I asked my family about our past, doing so for the first time with the intention of actually hearing the answers. What happened to my grandfather's siblings and parents who disappeared, and why it is that my grandmother said that she no longer believed in God after the war. But my mother does not know, or does not want to talk about the details, and both my grandparents have passed away.

There are no answers, and in a way, knowing the details does not matter anymore. I realize that my whole life I have striven to escape the limits of my nation's history, to transcend and define myself outside my Jewish identity. But there, in the camp, this attempt reached its end. A part of me, I have come to understand, will always possess an inherent fear that it could have been me standing at the fatal end of a machine gun, and I could have been one of the relatives who disappeared into oblivion and whose fate no one knows. As much as I have come to terms with my nation's past, it is a nation of Holocaust survivors, with its own inescapable heritage. And on this trip to Germany I have taken the first steps to begin to make peace with this legacy, which I now realize is a part of who I am.

My reflections in this essay were inspired by the works of Jean Améry, Hannah Arendt, and Giorgio Agamben.

The author in the stelae field of the Memorial to the Murdered Jews of Europe

Making History Public: Germany's Efforts to Remember its Past

Mary Rachel Gould and Rachel E. Silverman

Cities around the world continuously engage in acts of public notification about their pasts. City planners and government officials make decisions about who and what to commemorate, and in what manner this commemoration should take place. French Anthropologist Marc Augé suggests that it is in public spaces, specifically the urban city, where the story of a place is narrated for tourists and locals. Augé contends, "Every town or village not of recent origin lays public claims to its history, displaying it to the passing motorist on a series of signboards, which add up to a sort of 'business card.'"[1] Every city and state has events, people, and places they are proud of and want to display. Statues, monuments, and plaques adorn streets, parks, and town centers paying homage to the past. As a traveler, these sites become "must see" locations. For locals, these structures become defining characteristics of their neighborhoods and cities. Statues, plaques, and monuments become the physical manifestation of a point in time (a person, an action, or an event) that is deemed worthy of remembering. The history of people and place is inscribed on the city streets, where personal and public triumphs and tragedies have occurred.

As Augé notes, history is not hanging on the wall of a gallery, printed on the page of a book, or on display in a museum. History is on the sidewalks, brickwork, green spaces, and buildings that constitute the cities we visit and live within. In a museum, library, classroom, or book the story is protected and monitored by the authors (literal or figurative). In a museum the message is designed and overseen by docents and employees who are educated to help visitors understand the meanings of what they see and hear. On the streets there are no interpreters, no teachers, no "official" translators, there is just the object and the viewer. How does a city tell its history, when the story is often too complex for words? How can city officials ensure that the message of remembrance will be understood? On the street, who will ensure that history is remembered and not ignored or forgotten? The questions we ask here are questions that Germany's citizens, political leaders, and city planners have pondered for decades. How citizens of Germany and the German government have answered these questions is a testament to their efforts to

1 *Marc Augé, Non-Places: Introduction to an Anthropology of Supermodernity (London: New Left Books, 1995), 68.*

remember their past, and the extent to which they have made an effort to remember was evident to us as we traveled through the capital city of Berlin.

While it is easy to understand how a city or town would want to publicly commemorate a proud past, what about the places with tragic histories? How should traumas be remembered? How does a nation publicly present a past that cannot be glorified? How does a city lay claim to and remember a past that it is not proud of? Does it? Should it? Should an event such as the Holocaust be remembered in a public manner? More specifically, and the question that serves as the focus of this essay, we ask: how should Germany publically commemorate the places where genocide began?

Participating in the Germany Close Up program offered us the opportunity to experience for ourselves the efforts of the German government and citizenry to memorialize, and not glorify, the past. Through our own eyes we were able to see the way Germany (and specifically the city of Berlin) publicly remembers its past. Given what we saw during our time in Germany we believe the title of the program (Germany Close Up) is not only fitting and appropriate, but also subtly foreshadowed the experiences we had in Berlin. On each of the nine days of our visit we saw Germany from a unique and "close up" vantage point. We believe that our experience in Berlin was specific to the Germany Close Up program, in that we would not have seen Germany in quite the same way if we had designed this trip ourselves or participated with another group of "cultural tourists." Many of the sites and details that we were shown on our trip could have been easily overlooked or not rendered as meaningful had we not had our guides to bring us close enough to see them. Over the course of our travels we infrequently saw a billboard or mural sized tribute or remembrance to the Holocaust or survivors. More likely, we saw small and relatively unassuming memorials to the past. Many of these memorials and signposts required close attention and observation.

The need to look closely became most evident on one of our first walking tours through Berlin, a walking tour titled "Empty Space? Don't Trust the Green Grass!" As our guide, Dr. Pruin, pointed out a set of what we soon learned were "stumbling stones" many of us realized the significance of looking for and finding the small details that we would "stumble" upon during the course of our trip.

These tile-sized brass plaques, created by German artist Gunter Demnig and found on the sidewalks of Berlin and other cities throughout Europe, stand as markers to the victims of the Nazi terror. The four-by-four inch plaques are found in Austria, Germany, Hungary, and the Netherlands outside the homes and businesses of stolen lives. Since 1997, over thirty eight thousand blocks have been laid in the ground by Berlin native Demnig and his helpers. Demnig receives names and information from individuals and also from a database of victims found at Yad Vashem in Jerusalem. When Demnig acquires a new name, he constructs a four-inch concrete cube, which is then covered in a sheet of brass. The brass cover is engraved with the individual's name, year of birth, and, if known, the dates of deportation and death. Most common on the stones are the words, "Hier Wohnte" ("Here Lived").

Some say these stones are disrespectful to the dead; that walking on or over a person's name is disrespectful to their memory. Others think that these small and present reminders continually honor those who were lost. These stones encouraged our group to have critical conversations and discuss the act of remembering from both of these perspectives. The stumbling stones were one of the elements of our trip that could have been overlooked had they not been pointed out to us. Once they became present, we began to see them throughout the city. At times it seemed like we were all looking at our feet, trying to spot the next golden reminder in the sidewalk. At each stone we would stop, read the name(s) of the victim(s), and pause for a moment. Each stumbling stone in the city became a point of reflection for our group. These small markers were meaningful points of remembrance.

In contrast, the New Synagogue in Berlin was a much larger point of remembrance, one that not only provided us with the history of Jews in Berlin but also a present-day way to navigate the city and find our hotel at night. Our hotel was only a short walk from the New Synagogue, in the former East Berlin, and on many occasions we found ourselves navigating our way home by simply looking to the skyline for the architecturally impressive structure. The size and beauty of the building, along with the blue historical markers all over the neighborhood, aided us as visitors exploring a foreign land. As Jewish tourists in Germany, the Synagogue was not only a place to examine Berlin's past but also a point of reference for our present travels. The site fulfilled our need for positional orientation as well as our parallel need for historical and contemporary information. The New Synagogue was also a cultural point of reference for our group. In a rather ironic way, we all knew that once we saw the Synagogue we were headed in the right direction and were close to the hotel (our home away from home).

Only a few blocks from the Synagogue is an art gallery; during our time in Berlin an exhibition on James Brown was showing. Along the same road in the opposite direction is a museum dedicated to The Ramones. The contrast between the history we learned inside the Centrum Judaicum and the choices of music-based art all around us tells a story of Berlin's past as well as its present, and the juxtaposition reflects a city steeped in a dedication to remembering the past, but forging ahead into a globalized future. In a similar way, the armed guards standing at the archway entrance of the Synagogue also tell a familiar story – both of past and present fears and injustice. The closeness of our hotel to the Synagogue was a daily reminder of the modern trajectory of German culture and how contemporary Germany refuses to forget its past. Furthermore, our daily traversing of an area where Jews once lived, one now occupied by less traditional residents and tourists, provided ample time to closely examine how the past exists within the present. Once a Jewish neighborhood, the area surrounding the Synagogue is now a trendy district of bars and shops. The remnants of pre-war, Jewish life in Berlin were at times invisible to us; if it had not been for the help of our guides these small yet important details may have gone unnoticed.

Throughout our trip, it was the micro-details that elicited the most emotional responses. One example we can never forget was during a day-trip to the town of Wittenberg. Visiting the home of Martin Luther was a treat for all of us who had learned the history of his Thesis in our high school history classes. After almost a week of traveling through Berlin it seemed everyone was excited for a chance to visit places not part of Nazi history. The tour of the town took us through the church where Luther's infamous posting occurred; we explored his home and pre-Thesis life. Our walking tour through Wittenberg also took us to a memorial to the Holocaust, another remembrance set in stone and golden in color. This remembrance, a flat brass sculpture embedded in the cobblestones, sat on Jüdenstraße (Jews' Street).

The brass was molded as four panels, appearing to be separated by a golden liquid pushing through its cracks. In a square shape around the brass, was black stone with the words "From the depths, the truth will emerge," inscribed in both Hebrew and German. For quite a while we all stared at the plaque. The way the brass was bubbling through the cracks was striking and powerful. Our attention was diverted as we were directed to "look up." It was in this moment that we were brought face-to-face with the tension of remembrance. Above the memorial on the street, on the highest corner of the adjacent building, sat an antisemitic stone carving. The image was of a

Rabbi sucking the teat of a pig. The image immediately changed the tone of this experience. Our group was silent and it was apparent that there was a collective feeling of hurt and anger amongst our friends. The position of the somber memorial under the offensive stone carving created the space in which we stood, a space which mixed the past and the present, a space in which we reflected on the history of Jews in Germany and Germany's treatment of Jews. Then, without warning, someone started laughing. Soon, we were all laughing, and what we were laughing at had nothing to do with bubbling brass or pigs in stone.

To our left, under a large pine tree was a small brass plate. Engraved on this plate was the word "Sorry." This one little word changed the mood of our group, in this moment and for the remainder of our trip. Not even our tour guide in Wittenberg could tell us about this placard. She admitted to the group that this was the first time she had seen this sign. Although we do not know the designer's intentions upon placing the marker, as a group we almost felt it was placed there for us – or for a group such as ours having a similar unsettling experience. This one small symbol spoke loudly to our group.

Although we found great humor and irony in the sign, we also found it representative of our visit and our experience in Germany. This sign clearly signified the overwhelming sense of what we were experiencing – that the nation desires to publicly recognize and reconcile with its past, but that the public presentation of such efforts is complicated. The sign also allowed us to laugh, something we did a lot of on our trip. Laughter filled our trip. The small "Sorry" plaque gave us a reason to laugh during such a sad and tense moment, and laughter provided reprieve from our feelings of anger, hurt, and confusion. Our trip was laden with feelings of remorse and uncertainty brought on by the sights we were exposed to and the topics we were addressing. At the same time our trip was also filled with joy and laughter and our ability to find humor throughout difficult experiences. Laughing as a group created intimate bonds as we negotiated our proximity to the past. Laughing provided an outlet for our critical examinations. Laughing helped us negotiate the pain of remembering. Laughing was the source of much delight. Laughing not only brought us close to each other but closer to understanding modern Germany.

Throughout the week in Germany we were asked to notice a mix of past and present. The modern and historical sides of the nation allowed each

"Sorry" plaque in Wittenberg

participant to question the place Germany holds in today's world. The bonds built within our small group allowed us to ask each other many difficult questions. Questions such as *why* and *how* come first, then come the more specific, more nuanced ways of thinking. It was during these conversations, which mixed tears with laughter, that we were able to discuss our personal perspectives on German-Jewish, German-U.S., and German-Israeli relations. It was clear we all had our own opinions and insights to offer each other; the closeness of our group allowed us to express our thoughts as honestly and openly as anyone could hope. What this trip offered us was a space and a time to have these conversations. This trip provided a setting that encouraged us to talk about topics we might not otherwise engage in. With the backdrop of Germany/Berlin in each of our conversations, our point of reference was always the history that surrounded us, and the remembrances that were on every corner of the city. Through discussion and exploration we were brought close to each other and close to modern Germany. Our experience in Germany was about finding the hidden moments that connected us to a traumatic history that will forever be a part of our collective story as American Jews, and at the same time finding the ways in which we can continue to move forward, finding comfort and maybe even a moment of laughter.

Conversations, tragedies, triumphs, and laughter are what define the Jewish experience. What we were offered in Germany was an opportunity to experience each of these in the past, the present, and the future *Close Up*.

More Questions than Answers

Caroline Kessler

No one in my family is a Holocaust survivor. My mother is a lapsed Catholic and my father is a lapsed Conservative-turned-Reform Jew, whose grandparents emigrated from Ukraine during the pogroms. I grew up in a suburb outside Baltimore, where I was one of a handful of Jews. Growing up, my brother and I went to Hebrew school on Sundays, dreading even the relaxed Reform education we were receiving. As was expected, I made bat mitzvah and went through confirmation.

All this is to say that I had no emotional connection or familial ties to Germany. The most exposure to Germany that I had was learning about World War II in my public school history classes and learning about the Shoah in Hebrew school. My view of the country was narrow, focusing only on the years 1933-45. While I knew rationally that there was much more to the country than its darkest period, I couldn't move beyond this negative impression.

But that was part of the reason why I wanted to go to Germany in the first place – to be proven wrong, to find out what the country was really like today, if they had distanced themselves from their past.

*

In a way, I was proven wrong. Through the countless meetings, lectures, tours, and conversations with Germans and Israelis and Americans and Canadians, my mindset started to shift. I began to see Germany for its rich history and varied landscapes. Previously, when I met someone from Germany, something in my stomach turned over. I didn't let this unease show on my face, but I couldn't help but wonder: *Where were your grandparents during the war? What were they doing?* As unfair as I knew this was, to blame a current generation for the crimes of their grandparents, it was a reflexive reaction, one that was ingrained by years of learning about the Holocaust, of reading *The Diary of Anne Frank* and *Number the Stars*. Now, when I meet a German, especially one close to my age, I feel a sort of strange kinship.

*

But my reflection after the trip is more complicated than that reaction. As our group reflected together on the last night, I said that I was leaving with more questions than I came with, leaving with more questions than answers. And even months after the trip, I still have questions. Many of my questions and my wonderings revolve around this idea of collective guilt. I wonder if it's fair to blame today's generation for their grandparents' past.

During and after my experience in Germany, I wrestled with these questions in writing, because it is with words that I feel most comfortable. As a writer, I constantly think about how we express ourselves through language, either written or spoken. I obsess about language, turning over the same word in my head until it distorts into something foreign.

Memorial on the site of the former Jewish Home for the Elderly, Große Hamburger Straße, Berlin

The more I walked and bicycled around Berlin, the more subways I rode and windows I stared out of, the closer I got to some truth that I could only reach by being in Germany: this idea that guilt is linked to forgiveness. In writing about my experience, certain phrases kept cropping up, phrases that tried to succinctly summarize the phenomena surrounding the Shoah and the next generation: *collective consciousness, collective guilt, inherited guilt*. But I now wonder if these phrases have more than a lofty, academic kind of meaning or if they are hollow, superficial ways of trying to explain a complex, layered idea.

I wonder what the average German twenty-year-old thinks of the Holocaust, if he even thinks of it at all. I wonder what Berliners think of the Memorial to the Murdered Jews of Europe that squats in the center of the city, casting long literal and metaphorical shadows. I wonder what German children think when they see the “stumbling stones,” the small, dulled brass squares embedded within the cobblestones, bearing forgotten names.

But of course these visceral reminders indicate that Germans must think of the Holocaust. Even if it’s not every day, the reminders are beneath their feet, filling in their skyline, rising up from the city’s center.

*

Even outside Berlin, there is evidence of the country’s darker past. I wonder about the tourists who tramp through Sachsenhausen, taking pictures and laughing. I wonder why someone would want a picture of this kind of place. I wonder why it would not be seared into their memory, the stone ruins and wooden planks of the barracks. I wonder about the strangeness of the brilliant sky on the day we visited.

Again, these issues of remembrance and memorializing emerge. To preserve places such as Sachsenhausen requires considerable effort and resources. One of the things that surprised me the most about my experience in Germany was how many non-Jews were working in Holocaust-related fields – as guides at Sachsenhausen, as scholars in post-Holocaust studies, and running organizations such as Germany Close Up.

The idea that someone who had no personal connection with the Holocaust would dedicate part or all of their life to educating others was astounding to me. The issue of guilt comes up again here. Are non-Jews working in these fields to apologize for what happened? I dislike posing questions that I can’t answer, and I haven’t spoken to enough people to say for sure. The most interesting aspect is that both my participation in the Germany Close Up program, and the work that these non-Jews do as guides and scholars is completely voluntary. Today’s Jews don’t need to forgive or to alleviate the guilt of today’s Germans because there is nothing to forgive.

But, I wonder how I would feel if Germans didn’t seem to feel guilty at all. There would be a strangeness in that, especially because the tragedy is still somewhat recent. And yet, the Holocaust is something that is deeply ingrained in Germans. Especially in Berlin, it is difficult to escape the incredibly visual reminders, such as the Topography of Terror. But remembrance does not have to be equated with guilt. In fact, the remembrance in Germany seems to have a social justice aspect, an assuredness about it that indicates that something of this nature will never happen again.

While I had no connection to Germany and do not have survivors in my family, I still have an inherent connection to the Shoah because of my faith. Similarly, Germans have this same sort of connection to the Holocaust because of their culture. Just as the Shoah is not part of my day-to-day life, it may not be part of a German's life either. And yet, the Holocaust is deeply ingrained in both American Jews and non-Jewish Germans. We may not think of it every day, but there are memorials and museums and remembrance days that pull the tragedy to the front of our minds. Both groups learned about World War II and the Holocaust from a textbook. While these textbooks are written in different languages, we share the experience of this kind of learning.

These similarities make me wonder about the future, if German children and American children will have parallel experiences. I wonder how they will learn about the Shoah, without any survivors left. I wonder if watching a film or reading someone's diary will have any effect, will teach them anything about the past. I wonder how other American Jews my age feel about Germany, I wonder if they have similar prejudices.

*

I came to Germany thinking that I wanted to be proven wrong and that I wanted to find out what the country was truly like today. It's a challenge to attempt to understand the nature of a country's collective conscience after ten days. But at least it's a beginning. Again, I return to this idea that I left with more questions than I came with and more questions than answers. Some of these questions dissolved into tension – a tension between assigning guilt to a people, finding forgiveness, and wondering whether that guilt and forgiveness is even necessary today. After all the questions and conversations and writings and wonderings that stemmed from my time in Germany, I'm glad that I was proven wrong. I really look forward to the next time that I'm able to visit Germany, to continue answering and asking new questions.

Neue Synagoge, Berlin

Honoring the Memory of the Past

Liz Foreman

"You're going to Germany?

"I could – I could never go to Germany. I lived through the war and I just could never go there. Why are you going to Germany?"

"Why not?" I casually asked my 90-year-old great aunt Pat.

Even though I shrugged my shoulders, the truth was that I harbored a lot of the same hesitations. I wasn't exactly sure why I was going to Germany. As an American Jew born forty years after World War II, my Jewish identity was formed on notions of "Never forget the six million," and "Never Again." My main associations with Germany came from classes at school and movies I had watched, and focused on Nazi Germany. I knew bits and pieces about today's Berlin, and while with reservations, I was intrigued.

So, I went.

As I walked off the plane from New York into Tegel airport on a drizzly July morning, I felt tightness in my chest. Flight announcements came over the loud speaker spoken by an articulate female German voice. Even though the announcement told travelers of a flight to Copenhagen, I couldn't help but flash in my mind's eye to the main association I had with the German language. Holocaust imagery swam through my thoughts: a family boarding a train to an unknown destination. As the line of passengers filing out of the gate began to move, I stopped myself. No, no. I was in 2008 Berlin, in line for customs. I made it to passport control to meet a blue-eyed attendant. I wondered, as he flipped through the pages of my passport and saw the Israel stamps, if he would know that I was Jewish and refuse my entry. We exchanged glances, followed by the stamp smothering a nearly full page.

I was in.

I moved along to retrieve my bags. I found my fellow Germany Close Up participant and friend, Sara, and as we waited for our bags to come around on the belt, Sara whispered in my ear, "You know I couldn't help but think I was in the middle of a Holocaust deportation announcement when I first heard the voice in German." I could only chuckle, nervously embarrassed, when I told Sara I felt the exact same thing. We both looked around suspiciously to be sure no one heard us. Our bags came and we headed out.

On the first night of the program, I learned the context of Germany Close Up. I had been brought to Germany as an expression of thanks to the governments of the United States and Canada for the payments received under the Marshall Plan. I realized the trip was something different from just an exploration of the past. It was Germany taking responsibility for its actions and embracing modern progress. I wondered how I fit into this enormous equation.

My ancestors left various parts of Eastern Europe for the United States: Austria, Lithuania, Poland, Romania, and Russia. I know nothing of their reasons for coming to America, beyond the history of the Ashkenazic Jewish community. They likely escaped religious persecution and sought a better economic and social life for their children. Aunt Pat's words stuck with me. While she was born in America, I wondered what her older brother, my Grandpa Sam, would think of my travels to Germany. Sam immigrated to America at age six from Poland.

While he died before I was born, I always considered him my closest link to European Jewish life before the Holocaust. In one of the few existing family photos from Poland, Grandpa Sam is around two years old with shoulder-length blonde hair, standing with his entire family. Religious boys, like my grandfather, did not have their hair cut until the age of three; the rest of the family was dressed in religious garb. Grandpa Sam's father, absent from the picture, was already in America, working as a tinsmith and preparing to bring the entire family to America within a few years. When they eventually came on a boat to Ellis Island in New York, they would assimilate and discard some of their religious practices, taking on a more modern life, but never losing their Jewish identity and culture. I knew the German-Jewish community in those days was also characterized by a more assimilated practice of Judaism, steeped in Western belief and not dissimilar to what Grandpa Sam's family adopted in America. Embraced by this tremendous history in the name of the Marshall Plan, I suddenly saw the story of my own family against this background. Now was the time to put myself into the equation.

Once we began to tour Berlin and see the remnants of Communism, the beautiful new modern buildings, the cosmopolitan culture, and the unending number of war memorials – a grand mixture of past and present – I became much more comfortable. I stopped feeling the tightness in my chest when I heard German spoken on the street. In fact, I enjoyed pronouncing every word I saw written outside restaurants, on street advertisements, and on everything else I came across. I was impressed with the art and culture of the city and visited modern art museums whenever we had free time. Berlin's warm modernity softened my exterior as I explored pieces of history.

Early in the trip, the group visited the Neue Synagoge, or Oranienburger Straße Shul as it is also known, and learned of its history. Slightly damaged on Kristallnacht, the synagogue's fate had been sealed by heavy damage caused by Allied bombing during the war. Years later, restoration took place. We browsed restored artifacts from what remained of the main sanctuary. Left with a shortage of time and a large exhibit to take in, I became overwhelmed by what was lost. It was clear that this had been a vibrant Jewish community that prayed in a beautiful sanctuary. Suddenly I thought, "What became of these lives?" and I realized that many of them did not survive. To accept such a concept is not an easy thing to do. All my life I had learned about the lives that were lost during the Holocaust. Now I stood in a place where they gathered as a community and practiced Judaism, just as I do in New York.

Our group next moved on to the basement of the building, where the archives of the community are now kept. The archivist explained to us that pictures, community records, and many other items had been gathered from all over the world about the Jewish community that once called the Oranienburger Straße home. I was shocked by the volumes of information. These lives went back for centuries. The archivists are now working diligently to piece together as much information as possible about the community from people around the world. They are trying to piece together the families that once were.

The following morning, we visited the Jewish cemetery on the Schönhauser Allee. This cemetery was used by Berlin's Jewish community from 1827 until it became full and was officially closed in 1880. The people buried here, in many cases single families all together in one plot, were people who led full-fledged, thriving lives in Germany long before the days when the Nazis came to power. This cemetery was quite beautiful. It was full of rows of graves with ivy growing over the grounds. Although it was overgrown, this only added to its beauty.

I was deeply moved by the Jewish history which rested before me, in such a peaceful setting.

It was at this moment that I realized exactly why I was in Germany. I needed to see more of the Jewish past than just the Holocaust history that I already knew.

Old Jewish cemetery on the Schönhauser Allee, Berlin

The acts of the Nazis are completely unforgiveable. Nothing can ever make up for what was lost and nothing will ever make it right. These are notions that I was taught growing up and notions I still believe today. Aunt Pat's objection to a visit to Germany was rooted in this belief.

Memorializing the Holocaust and the bitterness of Germany's past should not stop us, however, from remembering the beauty of those who came before. It is they, too, whose memories were shattered when their descendants' lives were shattered. The ongoing initiative to build a vast archive of the community is a vital way to honor the memory of Jewish life. They are piecing together what existed as a resource for future generations. I needed to see this history, too, in order to understand a piece of the past.

Grandpa Sam's family's departure from Europe preceded the rise of Nazism only by a few decades. The lifelines of his family and those immortalized in the archives started out similarly. Standing two generations later in Berlin, it became tangible and personal to me.

When the group visited what remained of the Oranienburger Straße Shul, I wanted to be able to see the sanctuary and to say some prayers there.

A shortage of time during our visit did not allow this. I stayed in Berlin an extra day after the trip, and on my final Saturday, I went to Shabbat services with Eryn, another participant on my trip. I thought, perhaps, I would find an experience of the past and pray in this large sanctuary I had heard about. After going through security, we arrived at what is today's "main sanctuary," a small chapel-like space where the congregation prays together, probably holding a hundred people, at the most. The service was beautiful and full of a lot of spirit. I was surprised to find that it was a congregation affiliated with the United Synagogue of Conservative Judaism, the same movement with which I identify. I later learned that many congregants as well as the rabbi are converts to Judaism. The congregation, both in setting and people, was nothing like I thought it would be. A community grows today, with its own identity.

Eryn and I prepared to leave after the service was over. We both were still curious to see the main sanctuary, which we naively thought was where the service would be held. We spotted a man who had also attended the service, and asked him about the main sanctuary. He led us to a door that overlooked a large space. It was like we were looking down onto the main level of seats in a concert hall from the second or third level balcony, minus any evidence of current use. He pointed to where the women would have prayed and then to the bottom where the men would have prayed.

He then lamented, "It will never be again."

That tightness returned to my chest as those words rang through my ears. Speechless, I buried my curiosity; I would only be able to witness what exists today. The community I attempted to find was in the archives of the building. A new Jewish community was growing roots following a devastating history.

The following day, I flew home to New York. A few hours after landing, I went to Aunt Pat's apartment to visit her and my mom, Grandpa Sam's daughter, who was also in town.

Aunt Pat asked me several times, pointedly, "What is the sentiment of the people?"

I was not quite sure how to answer the question. I realized she was asking about the people who lived through the war, who perpetrated or stood as bystanders to the atrocities. She wanted to understand what had happened.

It was then that I realized that throughout my trip I, too, had sought to understand the past.

"It will never be again," resonated in my head.

Sitting in Aunt Pat's living room, I realized that the purpose of my trip was to join in moving forward. The Germans are taking responsibility for their actions and this was my opening to be a partner.

We must always honor and remember the memory of those who died at the hands of the Nazis. This continues to be illuminated in the community that rests in the Schönhauser Allee cemetery and in the archives of the Neue Synagoge.

The best answer that I could give to Aunt Pat lived in that small sanctuary in today's Oranienburger Straße Shul. The current Jewish community in Berlin, while small and markedly different from three generations ago, is growing. It is establishing a Jewish revival and defining its own identity. And in the rich Jewish tradition dating back thousands of years, new life is the ultimate sanctification of honoring the memory of the past.

Immersion in Living Waters: An American Rabbi's Journey Through Modern Germany

Rabbi Daniel Bogard

I'd been in Germany almost two weeks by the time I found myself shivering and wet, standing next to the thousand year old *mikveh* (Jewish ritual bath) in the city of Speyer. I had arrived in Germany a few days early to visit an old college friend, Michael, and then for the last week it had been the program. The program was made up of 15 or so mostly rabbinical students from Hebrew Union College, the only seminary for the Reform movement in America – a movement that began 150 years ago in Germany. We started the program with a week in Berlin, touring the sites with a strong emphasis on the *Shoah* and memorials to it. Most of these memorials I had seen five years before, when I had spent a few weeks on my friend Michael's couch, falling in love with Berlin.

I didn't want to love Berlin, of course. I didn't even want to like Michael when he ended up two doors down from me in our dorm at Macalester College. But almost because of it – because he was German and I was Jewish – we came together. He became one of my dearest friends, and we learned to embrace the discomfort of the *Shoah*. "Daniel," he told me one night, after a long conversation and perhaps a few beers, "I want to show you the camps." And so it was that four years later, I emailed him about a layover in Berlin on a flight to Israel. "Instead of meeting for a few hours," Michael said when I called to ask him, "why don't you stay for a few weeks?"

I loved Berlin, almost from the moment I landed. Busy, bustling, and warm; three things that don't normally go together in a city. Michael loves his country, but particularly loves Berlin, and he took me on a whirlwind tour of underground bars, outdoor music, and fantastic food.

While he was at work, I would spend my days at the Jewish sites throughout the city. I found myself surprisingly moved by the Memorial to the Murdered Jews of Europe, and astonished by the architecture of the Jewish Museum. But what most stuck with me were the Stolpersteine.

Stolpersteine – literally "stumbling stones" in German – are small, brass cobblestones that have been placed throughout Germany outside the homes where Jews once lived. On them are engraved the names of those who were taken away or murdered over the course of the *Shoah*. They are called stumbling stones because you are forced to encounter them, forced to stumble over them wherever you go in the country. I was amazed at a society that two generations removed continues to build memorials to their greatest shame, and moved at the willingness of the grandchildren of the Nazis to engage the sins of their forefathers.

"Stolpersteine"

It was at the end of that first trip when I finally decided to visit Buchenwald. I had been putting off going to the camp, but finally went to the station, bought my ticket, and was on an afternoon train to Weimar. I made it to Buchenwald too late, just as the site was closing down. I walked amongst the empty buildings, and tried to feel the ghosts in the walls, but soon I was ushered out. With no taxis outside, I ended up walking most of the way back to town until a man picked me up and drove me the rest of the way. I arrived in Weimar cold, dispirited, and a little anxious: this was the same walk that my ancestors had been forced to do when they too had arrived by train, and somehow when I came back, I expected to find the Weimar of 60 years prior. Instead, I stumbled into the central square into a scene straight out of a movie: the Christmas Market was up, and the cinnamon smell of the hot, spiced Glühwein was everywhere. The man who had given me a ride (and heard my sob story) insisted that he had to buy me my first few mugs of it – a debt that he happily allowed me to repay with the last few rounds later in the night.

I did end up making it to Buchenwald the next day, and I said my prayers, and a day later than I had planned, got on the train back to Berlin. I spent the ride trying to reconcile the two images: the unspeakable horrors of Buchenwald, and the welcoming, joyful Germany that I encountered at the Christmas Market. I had come to Germany wanting to hate it, and instead found myself missing the sights, the smells, and the people. Which is why when five years later the opportunity arose to go on a Germany Close Up trip, I jumped at the chance.

I had seen most of the memorials we were taken to in Berlin, but on my first trip I hadn't seen the vibrant Jewish life that has sprung up in the city. With over a hundred thousand Jews in Germany today, it has the ninth most Jews of any nation on earth.[1] Made up primarily of immigrants from the former Soviet Union, German Jewish life today is as varied as anywhere in the world. We spent Erev Shabbat (Friday Night) at a synagogue led by a German woman who had converted to Judaism and become a rabbi in Israel. Then, the next morning a few friends and I walked to another shul in Berlin, arriving just in time for the end of services. But the community was excited to have visitors, and we were invited to join the communal meal afterward, where much singing was done, and much vodka was drunk (these were Russian immigrants, after all...).

It was such a different experience, to see Jewish Germany not as a relic of the past, not as a thing to be memorialized and taught in history class, but instead as a living, breathing community. It was this mindset that I took with me as our Germany Close Up trip began to explore the country outside Berlin. We spent a day in Worms and Speyer, two of the three great cities (Mainz being the third) of Jewish learning in the Middle Ages. We saw the ancient graves of the great rabbis in Worms, and then finally made our way to the thousand year old *mikveh* at Speyer. Which is how I found myself, cold, shivering, and soaking wet.

The woman who showed us the grounds of the *mikveh* had been leading tours there for as long as many of us had been alive, but she was clearly very excited to have a group of rabbinical students. We prayed the mincha service (afternoon prayers) standing on the grounds where for most of the last millennium, the community shul had stood. She then took us to the *mikveh*, built underground so that it drew its living waters from ground-water. This

1 *Jeffrey Peck, Being Jewish in the New Germany (New Brunswick, New Jersey and London: Rutgers University Press, 2006), 41.*

is what had saved it when the Nazis came to power: it had been boarded up and used as storage. And so there it was, still a kosher *mikveh*, built by my ancestors a thousand years before, and it felt like it was calling out to me. Which is when I turned to Jack – a friend and fellow trip member – and together we asked if we could get in – if we could immerse ourselves in the waters.

The tour guide was so excited at the idea that this sweet, elderly woman literally ran back to the main office to ask permission. She came back smiling ear-to-ear, and clutching a towel that she had found for us, apologizing that she only had one for us to share. So Jack and I went in, we undressed, and then one at a time, we immersed. The water was freezing, the kind of cold that makes your teeth rattle and your lungs feel like you can't catch a breath. But it was amazing. In immersing, we became a part of our own history, and in doing so claimed a part of living Germany as our own. Above ground, we focused on the torn down remains of a thousand-year-old Jewish civilization that had been utterly massacred by the Nazis. But underground, coming out of the *mikveh*, we felt very much a part of the Jewish Germany that was very much alive.

The *Shoah* may have dealt an irreparable blow to the chain of Jewish history in Germany, but there are those working every day to add the next link: the non-Jewish tour guides we had at the memorials, who work to ensure that every German is aware of his or her history; the Russian immigrants with whom we spent Shabbat, who are focused on creating a contemporary, vibrant Judaism for their children in Germany; and the Germany Close Up staffers, whose hard work and remarkable dedication allowed a group of American rabbinical students to come and bear witness to the Jewish world that is taking root once again in this land.

Knowing Olli

Kerry Chaplin

Oliver – I later learned to call him Olli – is physically imposing, tall and wide, with a shaved head, which made him immune to walking in the rain without an umbrella. No hair to mess up, he said. He is studying to be a teacher, taking courses in history and theology, lives well outside Berlin itself, and shuttles to the city for classes and work. His formidable appearance uniquely qualifies him to be a bouncer. On the morning we met for coffee, he had slept only two hours, since he had finished work at 5am and returned both home and back to the city by train before meeting at 10am. Our conversation, the one we were about to have, was very important to him.

The first time we met, he and I and thirty other students, both Americans participating in Germany Close Up and Germans studying at Humboldt University, ate dinner together. Our table of six talked about Martin Buber, whose *Prophetic Faith* we had studied together during a Humboldt University course earlier in the evening – what does it mean, after all, that the Messiah should be godlike, but manlike? – and the differences and similarities between and within Protestant and Jewish theologies.

With one man, who lacked in general a sense of tact, I talked about the Shoah, which he seemed to write off as an unfortunate event in a series of unfortunate events enacted against the Jews. "There were, of course, many shoahs before it." In order to respond as consciously as possible, I intellectualized the discussion, pointing out that those were tragedies yes, but the Shoah for its industrialization of mass murder was, in fact, different, and only it is the Shoah. He continued to press my point, but eventually had to eat his soup. Where is the line between simple ignorance and antisemitism?

Throughout the discussions at our table, Oliver was quiet. He listened, interjecting a few times to say only that his English was poor. Not until the Jewish students were saying the prayer after a meal and I was showing the Hebrew text to the Humboldt students did he speak more than a few words. He translated the Hebrew to German for his classmates. And he asked me about the ritual itself – how often we say these prayers and why certain parts are said out loud and others are said quietly.

As we left the dinner, I encouraged him, "Your English is really very good. I wouldn't say so if it weren't true." He was embarrassed and self-denigrating, and I asked him for his contact information so that we could stay in touch. He paid his bar tab, and shared what he had likely hoped, but feared to share all evening: he had never before met Jews.

"What did you think?" I asked him with a smile.

He said, "Well, it's strange." He paused. "My grandfather was SS. He worked in the death camps."

I suppose I should have been more stunned, shocked, speechless, uncomfortable, but I was instead curious. "Did your grandfather tell you that?"

"No."

"Did your parents tell you?"

"No."

"How did you find out?"

"I opened a drawer and there was a picture of my grandfather – in uniform."

"How did you feel?"

"I was shocked."

We reached the last shared street corner on our walk out of the restaurant, and we stopped. Clearly, we needed more conversation, each of us from the other, if only to know what it was that we sought from one another. I suggested we get coffee later in the week. He must have liked the idea because before I could email him to set up a meeting, he emailed me.

And so Friday morning, Olli and I met at a train station and walked to a nearby café, which though he didn't live in the area, he remembered from another student gathering. It was a different café than he had remembered. "Things in Berlin change so fast," he said.

Neither of us had intended to talk for more than an hour and a half at most, so when he checked his watch four hours later, each of us was surprised. We talked about American politics, German politics, and finally about his family. "Do you think," he asked, "that we are responsible for the actions of our ancestors?" He looked at his third coffee as he asked.

The responsibility of both asking and answering the question was palpable. Was I, a Jew with no known familial ties to the Holocaust, to speak for all Jews? Was I being asked for absolution? For a reprieve from the certain weight of his uniformed grandfather sitting on his shoulders? I answered more quickly than I expected: "No, I don't think so. But it does make us responsible for the memory of their actions."

"Wishing Tree" installation at the Jewish Museum Berlin

I am still concerned that this answer is somehow illegitimate for its singular reliance on memory. Both during our organized Germany Close Up tours and during my own exploration, memorials spotted Berlin's city life. Whether a rarely recognized memorial turned park, an often visited garden of stone blocks, or sidewalk stones with the names of those murdered, memory of past actions, of the painful pieces of the German narrative, weigh down the collective psychological state of Germans. As a result, some Germans embrace a guilt that passes into philosemitism, others ignore what would otherwise be an overwhelming pain, and the rest fall somewhere in between, uncertain of the appropriate emotional reaction.

While Germans build external memorials, Jews build internal ones, clinging to the Shoah as the defining source of modern Jewish identity. The fear of erasure promotes a selective memory, highlighting a narrative of victimhood, rather than one of strength. Jewish Shoah education demands we remember the number 6,000,000, but rarely discusses freedom fighters, or tells the story of the Berlin women who successfully protested the expulsion and murder of their Jewish husbands, saving their lives.

In both narratives, German and Jewish, the weight of memorials affects our abilities to move forward. We become stagnant, so consumed with our own pasts that even in the present we lose sight of the future in order to reenvision bigger and better memorials, like that at Sachsenhausen or the recently renovated Yad Vashem. Simultaneously, we look for ways to leave the cycle: "Do you think we are responsible for the actions of our ancestors?" Olli asked.

Though I expected Olli's question from at least one of the Germans we would meet, and I expected to offer the answer I gave, I had hoped my experience during Germany Close Up would change my pre-formulated answer to address the emotional depth of the question beyond memory. Certainly, memory is important. But after the Germany Close Up experience, I am certain that memory alone is just as detrimental as it is necessary. In the future, I hope to understand how to communicate responsibility beyond memory – beyond victimhood, beyond monuments, and in spite of family silences.

Maybe Olli can help.

Tensions

Rabbi Maura Linzer

I was anxiously awaiting my 20th birthday. Just as my grandparents had purchased a car for my brother two years earlier, it was finally my turn. I felt like the luckiest person in the world. I remember my Zaidie's (grandfather's) admonishment, "You can pick any car that you want – *but* it cannot be manufactured by a German company."

Summer and winter childhood vacations spent with my grandparents in Miami were greeted with much anticipation – hours by the pool, home cooked meals, and naps lying peacefully in the arms of my Zaidie. As I grew older, though, I realized that my Zaidie did not sleep soundly. I questioned my mother, who revealed that the cause of his restlessness was post traumatic stress from his service in World War II. I often wondered about his nightmares that replayed over and over every time he closed his eyes.

When I graduated from college and decided to pursue rabbinical ordination, my Zaidie was immensely supportive, because he fervently believed in the necessity of engaging the next generation of American Jewish leadership. Meanwhile, he had become active in the Jewish War Veterans and was beginning to come to terms with his own past. My Zaidie had mixed emotions regarding my participation in Germany Close Up. He understood that it was vital for young people to witness the atrocities committed by the Nazis; however, this required traveling to Germany and supporting its economy.

I decided to participate in the program, both for the experiences that it promised and in the hope that it would provide me with clarity regarding my Zaidie's experience. I arrogantly assumed that I understood modern Germany as an intellectual topic because my father was a lecturer of Holocaust studies at a local university. Additionally, I had regularly attended community-wide *Yom Hashoah* programs and had guided Reform Jewish teenagers throughout Poland during the previous summer. It had never occurred to me that Germany could be defined by something beyond *just* the Holocaust.

When I received the trip itinerary, I learned that I would be traveling to the same region where my grandfather had spent significant time during and after the war. The itinerary included locations where my Zaidie served in the 6th Armored Division under General Patton's command in October 1944, the place where he served as a Military Policeman following the war, and Buchenwald, the concentration camp that he helped to liberate. I will never forget his words, "When we arrived at Buchenwald, the crematorium was still smoking." Despite my participation in the program, I had made a personal commitment not to enjoy my trip. I had resolved to travel to Germany to observe, with my own eyes, what the Nazis did to my people so that I could impart the story to my children and congregants when the survivors were no longer alive to share their accounts.

Arriving in Germany was surreal. Anxiety overwhelmed me once I landed and was surrounded by German voices. I distinctly remember the opening plenary session with the Germany Close Up staff members led by Anna Held, the acting director of the program. They urged, "There is no agenda for this program. We do not care if you walk away loving or hating Germany. What is most important is that you engage with Germany." These opening remarks permitted me the freedom to shape my own relationship with modern Germany and its history.

The days spent in Weimar, where my Zadie had served, were both meaningful and overwhelming. Although I had been to Babi Yar, Theresienstadt, and Auschwitz, there was something fundamentally different about my visit to Buchenwald. I was forced to come to terms with my Zaidie's story. What my Zaidie saw when he closed his eyes was no longer a mystery to me. I stood next to the same crematorium, strangle room, and watch towers that he had seen decades before. I could not help but imagine him there alongside me. I believe that my encounter with Buchenwald led to a deeper appreciation of my Zaidie's experience during his World War II service.

The entire trip was enlightening in many respects, revealing the way in which Germany has dealt with its dark past and how modern Germany has developed into a thriving nation and ardent supporter of the State of Israel. One exchange during my travels has left an indelible mark, drastically altering the way I engage with both contemporary Germany and its history. As a rabbinical student, I had the opportunity to meet with theology students from the Humboldt University of Berlin. I immediately felt at ease while interacting with these students who are also studying to become clergy. We spoke about our academic course work, theological beliefs, and our perceptions about our role as spiritual leaders of our respective communities. One German student in particular articulated the way she confronts the Holocaust, both personally and theologically, and she spoke intently about generational guilt. She further explained that although her parents' generation never knew their families' stories, her generation, the grandchildren, demanded answers to their questions in an attempt to come to terms with the "sins" of their ancestors. She asked me, "Do you know the sense of American pride that you feel when the American flag flies? I have never known such pride. When our country's flag waves at soccer games and I hear our national anthem sung, I have to ask myself, 'Am I proud of what that flag symbolizes to much of the world?'" At that moment, I comprehended the profound sense of national guilt that many Germans carry with them on a daily basis.

Although I was keenly aware of the experience of the second and third generations of Jews impacted by the Holocaust in both Israel and the Diaspora, I had never stopped to consider the experience of second and third generation Germans. Perhaps I had never reflected on their perspectives out of ignorance. More likely, the "victim" rarely pauses to feel empathy for the perpetrator. This was a complete role reversal for me, trying to ascertain the sense of national German guilt.

I was shocked at my own overwhelming emotional response. As a rabbinical student, I had been taught in pastoral care courses to empathize and then to sympathize. Listening to a colleague's painful feelings of immense culpability, I began to allow myself to feel her personal pain in an attempt to understand her experience. My rational conscience began to intercede: How could I allow myself to feel her pain? Was my empathy an act of profound betrayal of my people's story, and of my grandfather in particular?

Following the trip, I deferred a year from rabbinical school to pursue an M.A. in Middle Eastern Studies at Ben Gurion University in Beer Sheva, Israel. I arrived in Beer Sheva and began taking my intensive Hebrew language course. I discovered that Ben Gurion University had a relationship with Heidelberg University and that the language program was filled with German students. One day my teacher reported that one particular German student's grandfather had died, and she suggested that students reach out to her. Aware that I was a rabbinical student, the teacher pulled me aside and asked me to assess this student's well-being. The student came to class in the afternoon and, after a brief exchange with her in which I could sense her anguish, I invited her to dinner.

At dinner, she shared a bit about her grandfather and her deep sense of loss. We made plans to get together the following day and, before I knew it, we were spending every day together. Over the course of the semester, I learned that she had participated in Action Reconciliation Service for Peace in Haifa and was very knowledgeable about Judaism, Hebrew, and Israel. Immediately, we came to the realization that we had much in common; nevertheless, I still felt some lingering distance between us. I found myself continually questioning her motivation to study Jewish culture and religion.

During my regular phone calls home, I found myself sharing increasingly more about our burgeoning friendship with my family though never expressing my inner turmoil. I wondered whether this friendship was an act of negation of my family's experience and betrayal of my people's past. I constantly felt pulled in multiple directions.

The Germany Close Up program taught me that it is essential to openly discuss these issues, as both sides have residual psychological trauma associated with the Holocaust. It is only through honest and open dialogue that one can hope to come to terms with one's own inner struggle. We began candid conversations about the experience of being a third generation German and her understanding of the Holocaust in the German national conscience. Being open about my feelings allowed me to both cope with my own internal conflict as well as build a sense of trust between us.

The level of comfort and stability that we had achieved in Israel was shaken when I traveled to meet her in Germany. The purpose of my visit was to await the arrival of teens from America to lead them on a tour of the downfall of the Jewish European communities. Following days of workshops in Israel on the topic of the Holocaust, Germany's role in the murder of millions of Jews was particularly salient for me. I believe that I was feeling more vulnerable, more alert, and more suspicious of Germans than I had been the last time we had seen one another. Meeting me at the hotel reception desk, she began conversing in German to the clerk. Suddenly, I felt uneasy hearing her speaking German for the first time in her own country, removed from the superficial feelings of safety that Israel and the university community had once provided. Armed with the knowledge that it is essential to speak openly and honestly about my feelings of anxiety, I was able to verbalize to her my innermost thoughts. Our mutual openness made me aware of the source of my discomfort and, with her support, led to a resolution of such feelings.

Over the course of our friendship, I have accepted that this sense of internal agitation and conflicting personal and familial commitments has become one

Ground inlay at the Jewish Cemetery Weißensee, Berlin

facet of our relationship; however, this is not problematic if we can create an open space for dialogue without judgment, using the Germany Close Up philosophy as a guide for building this relationship. This has allowed for a deep friendship to develop between two people who unexpectedly share much in common. Driven apart by our grandparents' generation, yet brought together by the death of her grandfather. A friendship formed in the sovereign Jewish State between two grandchildren of World War II – one German and one American. This tension and irony has also led to a deep and vibrant relationship, rarely found elsewhere, made possible only by Germany Close Up.

Fragments of a Journey

Simon Goldberg

"And above all, watch with glittering eyes the whole world around you because the greatest secrets are always hidden in the most unlikely places."
Roald Dahl[1]

Prologue

If you want to know the truth, I never dreamt I'd ever travel to Berlin. I grew up in war-torn Jerusalem during the time of the first and second *Intifada*. As a child, I became well-acquainted with notions of antisemitism and contempt – forces I struggled to grapple with, and often failed. Once I was old enough to understand the horrors of the Holocaust, I wanted nothing to do with Germany. This was not only a result of the anger I had come to accrue. Nazi crimes were unforgivable, yes, but so was backstabbing my people – the Jewish people – a targeted minority that has been persecuted for thousands of years. Opening my heart to reconciliation would constitute betrayal, I sensed. And so I closed it, self-assuredly. Of course, I did not know any Germans then: my attitude towards Germans was a reflection of the collective memory echoed in my surroundings. So perhaps it's fair to say that when, on a summer evening in June, 2010, I decided to board a Berlin-bound plane, anxiety held me in a tight embrace.

Where the past meets the present

I remember arriving dazed: partly because I knew not what to expect from a modern-day Berlin; partly because I had not slept the night before; mostly because I was in Germany. The airport; the sights; the black, the red, the yellow; it all became very real, very soon. As we strolled out of the terminal and first turned our gaze to the German landscape, I experienced internal confusion. Simon to self: If I had been alive then, would I have traveled to Berlin in 1945? Would I have traveled to Berlin in 1950? No. The pain would have been too overwhelming, too near. I would have had no chance to grapple objectively with what had been done, what had been left undone. And I would have had the right to feel that way. But could my mere presence here, even in 2010, constitute recognition and validation inappropriate in and of itself? Am I voicing an affirmation of the German government, perhaps consenting that it has handled properly its Nazi past? Am I forgiving? Forgetting? Do I have a right to do either?

1 *Roald Dahl, The Minpins (New York: Puffin, 2009), 48.*

In Berlin, spaces are empty

They took us on a walking tour that traced the evolution of Jewish life in Germany. We began at the foothold of what was once the first synagogue in Berlin. We stopped at a Jewish cemetery where Moses Mendelssohn is buried. In large part, the cemetery was destroyed and today could be mistaken for a park. They told us not to trust the green grass. We didn't.

Time stops in Berlin. We were in Germany for what must have been a total of twenty-four hours when I turned to a friend I had known only for that short span of time and laughed with her: *It feels like we've been living here for a year.* A year in Berlin? You mean a lifetime? But at the same time, when our bags were packed and we were finally ready to leave, it seemed that time had flashed by; that we had lost track of how to keep track and that, simultaneously, we had been there for the longest and the shortest periods of time.

One day in Berlin, we discussed issues of guilt and the prospect, the possibility, of reconciliation. For the first time in my life, I challenged myself to dissociate the crimes of German grandparents from their children and grandchildren. Someone stated: *They cannot be held responsible for crimes they did not commit.* I stood frozen, initially shocked at the exclusion of modern German youth from complicity. An obvious statement to some, maybe, but it struck me as bold, bothering, and belligerent. I found it inconveniently truthful and remained amazed at its capacity to pierce all levels of my being. It had simply not occurred to me until it was articulated. I had harbored a bias of which I was unaware – I had been unwilling to become aware of it: *all Germans are alike*, I had thought. Though they are not.

And yet, I still fought the inclination to view Germany in a positive light. Commemorating the Holocaust was to remain a top priority, and in my heart that presupposed hostility, even rage, towards the country and people who, only seventy years ago, sought our annihilation. This was nothing I was supposed nor expected to admit, but as I reflected and considered my devotion to principles of honesty, feelings of deep emotional pain gave way to what I finally discerned as true: many Germans of today are good – they are as good a people as any.

Some graveyards are bigger than others

It was blisteringly hot when they took us to the dens of death.

We visited the Sachsenhausen Concentration Camp in Oranienburg. Starting in 1936, it existed largely as a forced "labor" camp for political prisoners and as an institution for the military training and development of SS men and women. That is, Sachsenhausen graduated them to Auschwitz. But there was no denying that the camp functioned also as an extermination site for "enemies of the state" and prisoners of war, among them 10,000 Red Army soldiers who were executed systematically by being shot in the back of the neck. Our tour guide showed us the crematorium, which was left almost entirely untouched. He told us that the history of mass-murder is the history of things you can no longer see.

In the suburbs of Berlin lies the House of the Wannsee Conference. There, on January 20, 1942, senior members of the Nazi administration met to define in writing the "Final Solution to the Jewish Question." We stood in that room – that same room where Adolf Eichmann and Reinhard Heydrich once stood and decided to destroy the Jews of Europe. They left no Jew out, sparing not even the Jews of Albania who numbered two hundred. Tears of agony and frustration accumulated under my eyes, waiting to explode.

An unlikely but likely Jewish future

Shabbat never ended in Berlin. For lunch on Shabbat afternoon, we split up and were hosted by local Jewish families. The couple that welcomed us into their home was warm and friendly. Their boy, Kobi, was on the lookout from his window on the second floor when he spotted us, a group of wandering Jews. Kobi was shy, and his lack of fluency in English brought joy to my heart: the only languages he knew were Hebrew and German. We chatted as we passed the salad bowls up and down the table. I asked him what his favorite subjects were in school and what he learns in Yeshiva. I was touched when I realized that this boy today has opportunities that existed – at best – as stolen dreams under Hitler's rule. Who would have ever imagined that in 2010, a young Jew in Germany would taste such freedom?

Today there are over 100,000 Jews registered in the general community in Germany. For us to have borne witness to such a thriving Jewish community – one that has risen from the ashes of the Holocaust – was extraordinary. Millions of our own died here, with prayers on their lips and faith in their hearts. And yet, we see tragedy intersect with hope as the past interacts with the present. What a thought to entertain in 1945: that *this* country would become the breeding-ground for the fastest growing Jewish population in the world; what a testament to our endurance as a people; what a victory over Nazi tyranny.

Rabbi Chandalov took us on a night tour of Leipzig following a pleasant dinner at the Tora Center with the local Jewish youth, the vast majority of whom immigrated to Germany from the former Soviet Union when the gates opened in 1989. Bellies full, we were introduced to a city with a remarkable history; a city home to the Battle of Nations monument, built to commemorate the defeat of Napoleon; a city where the first Jewish wedding in Germany was celebrated in over seventy years. The young Rabbi joked about how, given the community's size, he holds one or several positions at once.

Smiles blended with sorrow as he guided us to a canal and revealed the fate of the city's Jews during the Holocaust: rounded up by the river-end, the vast majority of Leipzig's then 12,000 Jews were deported to the East and sent to their death. Towards the end of the tour, we passed by a building that once functioned as a synagogue, but which was desecrated on *Kristallnacht* in November, 1938. In a treasured moment, the Rabbi paused and told us how he often recalls the legacy of his ancestors. Looking at the glowing moon, he marveled at his ability to recite Birkat HaLevana where they had once recited it.[2]

In darkness, there is light

It happened during our final hours in Berlin. We traveled to the German Resistance Memorial in the Mitte District, the historic site of the attempted coup on July 20, 1944. Standing in the courtyard, a pool of emotions rushed to my head, heart, and stomach. The plaque there was commemorating the life and death of heroic German officers, visionaries of peace and protectors of a Sacred Germany who sacrificed everything to save the world from Hitler's depravity. I felt chills run down my spine as I realized where I was standing. *This was the site of their execution by the SS – where the last of their efforts failed.* I saw these men deliberating as fears of risking their families for their own convictions peaked, but were subdued; when, in a cry of humanity against fascism, they planted an explosive in Hitler's East Prussian lair; when they were summarily shot to death by firing squads and in their last breaths chanted resiliently, defiantly, hoping together for a better German future.

I looked to my right and admired the courage and ambition of our German tour guide, Anna, who has dedicated her life to dialogue and who spends weeks at a time exploring her country's guilt and shame with various Jewish delegations. In her work, Anna has traversed boundaries of time and space.

2 *A traditional Jewish blessing over the reappearance of the moon, signaling the beginning of a new month.*

She set out to remove the barriers that needlessly separate us. Anna paved the road I had avoided. Anna glowed with life and progress. She dreamed, questioned, and hoped. Anna broke away from hate, and loved. It was then I saw clearly for the first time: young people like Anna represent the Germany of today. And tomorrow.

The author in the commemorative courtyard of the German Resistance Memorial Center, Berlin

Memory's call

We have to preserve hope in humanity. To achieve that, we must be willing to do our part in paving a road towards reconciliation and mutual understanding. Our task cannot be to accept forgiveness, for who are the German people of today to offer an apology and who are we – the Jewish people – to ask for one? We are in no such place. But if we fail to recognize the possibility for change in a country and a people, then we are ultimately guilty of the crime of prejudice. If we are to be expressive of ethics, we must lean back and forward at once; learn from history and establish it as a platform on which to build a better future. I turn one eye to the past, shedding a tear and screaming voicelessly in anger and desperation at all that was lost and my inability to comprehend.

I turn the other to the future.

The Irony of Time

Yehuda Rothstein

I grew up in an Ultra-Orthodox or *haredi* community in upstate New York. This community could be considered a refugee colony because it was originally a place where a disparate group of Ultra-Orthodox Holocaust survivors gathered to continue their pious pre-war European existence. None of my immediate family members experienced the Holocaust. It was only through the eyes of my friend, Aharon Simcha, that I first learned about this great tragedy.

When I was a child I learned something disturbing about my friend's grandparents – they were always in pain and there was nothing Aharon Simcha or anyone else could do to help them. In every moment, in every action, in every joy, and in every sorrow, Aharon Simcha and I could feel rigid scars etched into his grandparents' and parents' hearts. Aharon Simcha was born with a box full of darkness and he could not comprehend its contents.

When Aharon Simcha was a child, every night his elderly grandfather would retire to his study to be alone with God and his Torah. Some of Aharon Simcha's warmest memories included being wrapped in the comfort of his bed listening to the soothing and soulful chant of his grandfather reciting the Talmud. But sometimes, his grandfather's chanting turned to sobs: "To think of all the Torah study we lost...," he would tell us, "everyone is gone, lost and destroyed in *churban Europa*."

Rabbi Berel, Aharon Simcha's grandfather rejected the English word "Holocaust" and the Hebrew word "Shoah" – words associated with the social ills of Secularism and Zionism – to describe the mass "pogroms" against the Jews during the Second World War because he believed that it was the Zionists and the reform oriented *Maskilim*, through their secularism, atheism, and rebellion against God, who provoked the King of Kings to pour out his rage upon his special nation. Armed with this truth, Rabbi Berel, like some others in the community of my youth, instead used the word *churban* – a Hebrew word for destruction, loaded with theological significance, that invoked the memory of the annihilation of Jerusalem, its ancient temples, and the wrath of the exile that followed the sins of ancient Israel – to describe the horrors committed by the Nazis and their allies.

And then, as it normally happened, Ruchie, Berel's wife, would arrive in his study and admonish her husband. "Stop it!" she would command him, her words echoing throughout their home where I lay awake in bed. "Stop crying, Bereleh! There is no time for tears!" she would say shaking him with her words. "God does not want our tears," she would tell him before leaving him alone to his Talmud.

I never saw Ruchie cry or mourn. I only saw her build. Yet, I remember sleeping near Aharon Simcha and in the darkness of the night, hearing his grandmother's cries reverberate through the walls of her empty nest. "Nein!" she would plead in German, "Nein! Bitte!" she would beg as her daughter, Aharon Simcha's mother, tried to calm her. Her cries frightened us but there was nothing we could do to comfort her.

Aharon Simcha's grandmother refused to talk about her childhood and any attempt to broach the uncomfortable subject was met with stone cold failure. What was known was that each of her many children and grandchildren held the name of an exterminated family member and that each was a living memorial candle for the hopes and dreams of not only a traumatized family but an endangered people.

Theories abounded amongst Aharon Simcha's relatives about what had happened to Ruchie during the war. Shimon Dovid, the nephew of Aharon Simcha, and a year his junior, said she had been with the partisans. Fraydie Sorah, Aharon Simcha's aunt, said that Ruchie had been in a concentration camp and had been experimented upon. But the truth was that nobody knew for certain what had happened to Ruchie.

And yet, Ruchie would awake early each morning perfectly groomed and with a smile on her face. After Aharon Simcha would leave for school she would telephone each of her children and grandchildren inquiring of their well-being. She would plan community welfare projects and coordinate with the local *Bikkur Cholim* organization to visit the sick. While others slowed with age, Ruchie's energy and desire for normalcy only increased.

It was Ruchie's quest for normalcy that I believe, motivated her command that her daughter make her grandson be my friend. Ruchie was a tree without roots and it was exactly the deeply rooted normalcy of my family that she wanted Aharon Simcha to experience and which motivated her to make me a *"Ben Bayis"* (or regular visitor to her home). My family was not as pious, but we had living aunts and uncles, cousins and grandparents, great aunts and great uncles. For Aharon Simcha's mother and grandmother, there was something appealing, pure, and rare about a family without the scars of destruction. For all the ways in which my family was different, for all the ways in which we were not as prominent, we had something that their family would never have – a lack of cross-generational trauma.

I have since left the community of my youth. I have traveled and lived in some two dozen countries on four continents. I have studied Islamic law in Cairo, Egypt, and Torah in multiple Yeshivoth in Jerusalem; trekked through the dunes of the West African Sahara, and strolled through the gardens of Suzhou, China. Yet for all my openness, for all the way my human spirit connected effortlessly with those I met on my journeys, there was a certain disdain that I felt towards the nation of Germany. It was not a place I cared to visit.

No grandparents of mine died in the war but my grandfather's favorite cousin stopped returning his letters in the summer of 1941. Years later, when I visited Belarus I learned that this cousin and hundreds of our distant family members had been massacred in the fields of Tolochin by the Einsatzgruppen in the Belarusian countryside. My immediate family was not directly involved in the Holocaust, but as a Jew, I shared in the collective trauma of my people. I grew up with neighbors and teachers who lost their parents, siblings, and spouses during the Holocaust. The collective trauma of the Jewish people, of the experiences of Aharon Simcha, and his grandparents, although not in any manner comparable, became, and are, my personal trauma and experiences too. It is mind boggling to think that in less than a decade, one third of the Jewish people were annihilated simply for being Jews. Permanently carved deeply into my heart are Rabbi Berel's tears and pain, and etched into my soul is the obligation to remember and honor every person who was murdered by the Nazis and their allies. I can never forget nor can I ever forgive.

My recent trip to Germany on Germany Close Up, an American Jewish Committee program, showed me a very different Germany from the one I could have imagined in my youth. There is something unforgettable about meeting young and middle-aged Germans and observing firsthand how German society has wrestled and continues to wrestle with the legacy of the Holocaust. There is something inspiring about meeting the descendents of Holocaust perpetrators who, when they came of age, revolted against their teachers, parents, grandparents, and great grandparents, asking them with shame, anger, disgust, and pain, "WHAT DID YOU DO?!"

My trip to Germany reminded me of Rabbi Berel's use of the word *churban* to describe the horrors of the Holocaust. Meeting with many wonderful young Germans, seeing how German society has evolved over the past few decades, and understanding the larger implications of Nazi ideology, has reinforced in me the belief that the philosophy of *churban Europa* is too particularistic and limiting – not just for Jews but also for humanity. If we are to think of the Holocaust as *only* a *churban*, as *only* a Jewish tragedy, as *only* a catastrophe brought about by the follies stemming from the decline of Jewish life and observance, or by the Zionist pursuit of Jewish historical rights – then the Jewish people, and indeed the human race, are missing out on many incredible lessons.

I have thought long and hard about the lessons, which could be drawn from the Holocaust, and no doubt the lessons of this tragedy are many.

As a Jew, it is the lesson that the Jewish people, like any other people, must be masters of their own destiny in their own homeland. Although Jews must remember the particularistic lessons of the Holocaust we must simultaneously remember that within these lessons there is a universal message, which we have an obligation to share with others in *a universal manner*. And although it is true that the Jews were the primary victims of the Holocaust, the Germans its primary perpetrators, and that Jews uniquely suffered during the Holocaust, the Holocaust is not just a German and Jewish story – it is a human story. If we make the Holocaust only a Jewish story, then we prevent the rest of humanity, and particularly the Islamic world, from appreciating its countless lessons. The Holocaust was a *Jewish* tragedy, noted Elie Wiesel, but one with *universal implications*.

As an American, and proud member of a nation, which liberated Europe, I believe that the United States must never be silent in the face of genocide and totalitarian regimes advocating genocide. As the nation in which liberty was born, and which continues to strive to become an ever perfect union that is a model to the world, it is our obligation to support freedom, and to fight those that pursue genocide anywhere and everywhere. Mass murder, or threats of mass murder, can never be ignored or tolerated. As Jews and Americans, our obligation to fight genocide, in all its forms, is only compounded.

For humanity, the Holocaust poses difficult questions about our species. The crimes of the Nazis were so extensive, systematic, and unprecedented that the word genocide was created to describe it. How is it that a society evolved that could commit such horrors? How can we encourage the development of societies that embody life, liberty, and freedom instead of genocide and death? If humanity is capable of beautiful creations and yet also capable of such horrible nightmares, why can we not encourage the former?

I do not have the answers to these questions – but my trip to Germany has shown me that no matter where a nation might stand at a particular moment, no matter what darkness surrounds a society, something brighter and better can be part of its future. No nation is incapable of paving a better future for itself, no matter how seeped in evil it currently may be. People who live in nations with totalitarian and hateful regimes can look to Germany as an example that declares loudly that nations, with time, can reshape their destiny and society. We can make a better town, city, nation, and world if we try. Nations, like people, the prophet Jonah teaches us, can do *teshuvah*, meaning that they can, with work, repent for their sins. Those who do *teshuvah*, the Jewish sages teach us, are an example to others because they have within their past sage and painful lessons on which to draw.

Part of Germany's process of *teshuvah* is to take the lead in Holocaust education around the world. Germany must take more dramatic moves, politically and otherwise against Holocaust deniers and be the first nation, not the last, to respond to incidents of murder and genocide around the globe. It is precisely Germany's past experiences, which give it a moral obligation to be at the forefront of human rights leadership. If Germany wears its experiences, not as an eternal badge of shame, but rather as of sage experience; if it stands up against genocide around the world; if it defends the helpless with its entire military and economic might; if it acts for justice without consequence because it knows better than anyone else the destruction that inaction brings in the face of intolerance and hate, then perhaps Germany can one day find solace.

I have not spoken with Aharon Simcha in over a decade but I still think of him. I am certain that neither he nor his family would ever have agreed to visit Germany. There is too much pain, too much baggage associated with the German nation. But I wonder if Aaron Simcha and his family could accept the possibility that there exists a new generation of Germans who have painfully wrestled, and continue to wrestle, with their past. From what I remember of Aharon Simcha, I think that he would never have visited. Aharon Simcha's struggle, like those of his progressive German counterparts, is that of trying to wrestle with the phantom of a haunting past. The struggle of the millennium generation of Jews and gentiles, both Americans and Germans, is how to balance the importance of remembering the gross human failure of the Holocaust, within the unique and individual paradigm of its particularistic lessons, while at the same time, to forge a better future guided by the countless universal lessons found within this tragedy and only made clearer by the sands of time.

Signs of remembrance at the former concentration camp Sachsenhausen

Welcome Back

Rebecca Pedinoff

Coming to Germany for the first time was a lot like coming home to a place I'd never been before. At the same time, it was also entirely new and different from what I had expected. It's not that I arrived and simply became enamored with an exotic foreign culture, as travelers often do. Rather, it was a feeling that I already knew these people, the language, the food, and these places. This foreign trip was not like any other I've had because it was also intensely personal. Like many Ashkenazi Jews, I really don't know where my family originated except that they had been wandering around Europe for a number of centuries. Eventually they settled in Northern Germany and lived prosperously up until the early 20th century. Family stories recount the happy childhoods had by my grandparents in Berlin and Hamburg: centers of commerce and modern development. They were proud, cosmopolitan Reform Jews in the German tradition. Growing up as a second generation American, I was used to hearing my grandparents pepper their speech with German phrases, cook German food, and act in typically "German ways." At the same time, stories about World War II, the Holocaust, and escaping to America were also common during family gatherings. Even as a young child I knew that these very different stories did not sit well together. This caused me to have an extreme curiosity to see and experience the places of my grandparents' childhoods, as well as to figure out a way to reconcile the opposing narratives I was presented with.

My first step off the plane was strangely familiar: hearing my grandparents' accents all around me; recognizing the candy and food sold in the kiosks (Ritter Sport! The smell of bratwurst!); reading signs directing me to places that resonated with family history (Berlin, Charlottenburg, Tiergarten). It was wonderful and also disconcerting because I really had no idea where I was or how the transit system worked, which are typical feelings when one encounters a new place. I was clearly missing some information, or things had radically changed, or both. I suppose it was another paradox to add to my growing collection. The picture that I had of Germany was clearly historical, but now out-of-date. It was also a land made entirely of stories and for the first time it was becoming real. There were giant gaping holes in my knowledge of the country and its people that were quickly being uncovered and filled in.

The early days of the trip included quite a few tourist excursions where we visited the main sites and learned a bit of history. It was fascinating to be in the place where World War II began – to try to understand the circumstances that would allow a dictatorship to take power, the way the people lived at the time, and to see what was left from that era. There are still old buildings standing, mostly the ones made of stone. Many of the walls are blackened with age and pockmarked by the shelling that occurred so long ago. As an American, and a Californian in particular, this is an amazing and terrifying sight. We have no buildings this old or marked with war. There were also conspicuous absences of things, like the "hole" where the Schloß used to be in Berlin, now just foundations and an open field covered in snow. We laughed when the tour guide mentioned it, perhaps because we couldn't imagine a grand palace in such a forlorn spot. We could not comprehend the enormity of what had been lost. So much had occurred there within the last century, it is a miracle that anything was left at all. I wondered what it would be like to see this city through the eyes of my grandmother who grew up here, and if she would even recognize it. All throughout the trip I would come back to this theme of loss, as I would try to imagine how people dealt with the sorrow of the total destruction visited upon them.

In the space of what was destroyed, a thousand memorials have sprung up. I saw them everywhere – remembrances of the war, of communism, of the Wall and the separation. The frozen winter landscape at the time made the reflective atmosphere even more pronounced. Going to a concentration camp in -7°C weather was an experience I will never forget; much less fathom how anyone could have survived it. It was incredibly powerful for me as my first time at such a site. My journal entry for this excursion is short: "I don't know what to think." I still don't have a much greater understanding about this terrible chapter in history. It gave me a renewed sense that atrocities anywhere must not be allowed to continue, and that modern-day crimes against humanity are something we still need to fight. It was history made real.

It seems that Germans live with the horrifying every day, all over their cities, even in the lovely old countryside that is quiet now, but filled with ghosts. It is a mere block from the famed Brandenburger Tor to the Holocaust Memorial, from neoclassical grandeur to stark modernist simplicity, from historical greatness to overwhelming shame. I think this ubiquitous cognitive dissonance is a hallmark of the country, one that the people have mostly learned to cope with in a thoughtful way. I appreciated how the memorial itself was meant to focus on continuing dialogue and interpretation, as opposed to being just another heavy-handed memorial that "makes it easier for us to forget." As I was continually comparing my own culture with this new one, I wondered if America will one day be able to confront the dark chapters of her past with similar thoughtfulness. I am not saying that Germany has done perfectly in this respect, but considering other countries (including my own) I think they've done it admirably. Now that the majority of Germans are much too young to remember or even have been born before the war, I think they are going to be moving away from that process of constant remembering. Perhaps it is useful to move on, and let some old wounds finally heal. Not to forget, but to have some distance and perspective on the past in order to really move forward.

It helped to have a little "inside information" when looking around, to know that there had been unfathomable changes on the very spot where I was standing. For example, I visited the Goethe University in Frankfurt, and I know it used to be a U.S. Military Base only because my mother used to work there in the 1970s. I am sure she would barely recognize it now, just as I have a hard time believing that the Germany I saw was under American occupation not so long ago. The most striking places to me were those without restoration, where the rubble and the burnt-out hulls of buildings were left in place as a reminder of the destruction. While visiting the New Synagogue on Oranienburger Straße I noticed how, despite the lavishly reconstructed facade, they had left traces inside of the burning – like the bimah, with its melted metal inlay "dripping" off like molasses – as though time had been standing still all these years; as though the past had come to inhabit the present. Meanwhile, I noticed other restoration was total, like in Frankfurt where the old city square had been completely destroyed and then rebuilt in the exact same style. If I didn't know better, I would have assumed it was original. It almost felt like I was walking through a "theme park" of history. I guess much of Europe is like that these days. It is amazing that most of these restorations have only recently been completed, and many are still in progress. The healing process is long, indeed.

When thinking about Germany, we tend to focus on the 20th century only, but there is so much more history to encounter. I was amazed at seeing thousands of Roman artifacts in Cologne, unearthed from directly beneath the city itself. Then, above that museum rises one of the grandest gothic cathedrals in all of Europe. The amazing cultural and historical breadth was not lost on me. I saw two ancient mikvehs in Germany, which are some of my favorite reminders that Jews inhabited a place where there is otherwise no trace left. Modern Jewish life seems pretty nonexistent due to the fact that the Jews themselves are mostly gone. There are endless memorials, graves, and plaques – memories only.

Cemeteries are overgrown and empty of the living. I could tell a lot of money went toward the memorials and exhibits, but there were just not a lot of Jews around to see it. Most of the Jews in Germany now are immigrants from Russia with a different history and no real connection to the country, which makes me sad when I think of how my own family considered themselves to be so German before having to leave it all. I visited my great grandfather's old department store (or rather the spot where it used to be) on the Kurfürstendamm. I visited his grave in a very old part of the very old Jewish cemetery. I cleared away the sticks and ivy and placed a rock on his headstone, as my mother taught me to do. I took a similar pilgrimage to the house in Hamburg where my uncle was born, just to see it still there. These are real, tangible traces of the life that they had. I half expected to spot pictures of my relatives in the Jewish Museum inside the exhibit on the photographs and material culture of late 19th and early 20th century Berlin. Visiting these places, of which I had only heard stories before, was like getting back something, which had always been lost. I was getting back my past. Then we went to services at the Conservative synagogue with a woman rabbi, leading half-German, half-Russian services sprinkled with English. Afterwards, kibitzing with young German-speaking Jews from Berlin. Enjoying lox together! History be damned! Perhaps the most quintessentially new Berlin experience I had was spending all night at a dive bar, which happened to be owned and run by a crazy Israeli. I thought it was quite fitting.

Fusing the old and the new in Berlin is the Reichstag itself, war-ravaged stone surmounted by a hyper-modern dome. I was struck by the use of glass and mirrors in much of the newer architecture of the city. I think it is not so much a modern stylistic tendency, but a reaction to both the dictatorship and separation that Berlin had to endure for so long. A rejection of the opaque, massive, boxy aesthetics of fascism and communism in favor of light and transparency. With such a tumultuous past, it's not hard to imagine that people just want some clarity in their future. Despite the years many things were *still* in the process of being reconstructed, the rubble continuing to be cleared, the reconnection of East and West an ongoing process. I was amazed at how long this could take, and how the city went on in spite of this never-ending reconstruction. We learned the hard way that there is two of everything in Berlin due to the former East/West divide. I think this must be entirely unique for a city. When I heard that the East Side Gallery was on its second or third generation of paintings, I thought it particularly reflective of the palimpsest that is Berlin in general. The more recent history of Germany seems brighter, with an enthusiasm for technology and cultural pursuits.

There were so many new things to see, like the cinema during the Berlinale, and the "underground" graffiti art that everywhere turned bland concrete walls into outdoor art galleries. And of course the innumerable museums with excellent collections and meticulous labeling. Perhaps the tendency to document and memorialize is just one aspect of this greater appreciation for the organization and presentation of information. The restoration and citywide unveiling of the movie *Metropolis* was deeply moving. If there is one thing that really impressed me, it was the willingness of people to put so much time, energy, and funding towards social and cultural endeavors. It feels, well, civilized.

Glass dome of the German Reichstag building

Of course on the trip I also learned that Germany has its issues, like the ongoing problem of incorporating immigrants into mainstream society, and the regional differences, which will probably always assert themselves. It was in learning about these issues that I began to see Germany as a much more interesting and dynamic place, my knowledge becoming more well-rounded. And yet, there is still so much more that I want to do, so many regions and places that I did not get the chance to see. In the end, the trip gave me something that I had been searching for practically my whole life – my roots.

I really liked Berlin. It's not a typically beautiful city (at least not in the frozen winter), but I appreciated its aesthetics nonetheless. Sure there are grand buildings and beautiful European pedestrian walkways. But the old destruction, and new grunge and graffiti everywhere gives the city an undeniably imposing presence. It saves it from being a boring or otherwise squeaky clean Northern European city. Berlin is spread out and massive and flat. The baroque 19th century facades and the stale grey communist boxes bump up against each other with wonderful abandon. The still-recent legacy of separation and reunification is one of its saving graces. It is a city that remains very much still rebuilding and re-imagining itself. Maybe it doesn't quite know where it is going. The discussions and dialogues are still in progress. Like the country as a whole, it is flawed and modern and real. It is not as pretentious as other European cities of similar stature. Good and bad, high and low, cool and uncool exist together and punctuate each other in a sublime way. Like great fiction. But it's very real.

Heltzen

Adam Heltzer

I turned 28 on the flight from Boston to Berlin. Despite having never visited Germany before, I had cultivated a fairly vivid image of Germany and Germans. The most dominant images of the country materialized in black and white form, through grainy, disjointed film clips. The few German words I knew were *schnell, achtung, verboten.*

When I shared my plans to go on Germany Close Up with my family, my mother paused conspicuously before continuing, "...I could never go there, I just couldn't. I can't imagine being in that place."

My uncle chimed in, "I think you're very brave to go, but I have no desire to go there, whatsoever."

They themselves had not experienced World War II, but their parents had. From the sidelines of America my grandparents could do little to stop the horrors taking place. The result was a piercing combination of fear, rage, and powerlessness. These were the sensations associated with the Germany that reverberated through my parents' generation and still echoed noticeably in mine.

So when I was accepted into the Germany Close Up program and the reality of the trip sunk in, I wondered: Had enough time passed since the Shoah for me to reengage with the country? I felt like an emissary representing generations past, with instincts to both reject the Germany Close Up proposition outright and to approach cautiously, like testing new ground with an outstretched toe.

The twin concepts of redemption and forgiveness, nearly universal across faiths and cultures, loom large in Jewish philosophy. Each year on Yom Kippur we examine our own transgressions; it's the process of acknowledging our sins and owning the regret that provides the opportunity for rebirth. The evils perpetrated during the Holocaust tested the limits of these principles, but Germany's collective contrition in the years since encouraged me to take a step closer.

*

This was my frame of mind when I arrived in Berlin and checked into our hotel in Mitte. I was greeted warmly by the front desk clerk, tall, slim, and strong, with a classic Aryan look that came right from the World War II movies I'd grown up watching.

“Checking in for six nights Mr. Heltzer?”

Though my immediate pre-American ancestry hailed from various small towns scattered throughout Poland, Russia, Latvia, and Lithuania, my surname bears a German origin, likely from a centuries-old eastward migration across the European continent as Jews fled oppressive regimes.

As the clerk rounded out his greeting my ears perked up. There was something about the throatier “H,” the strong emphasis on the first syllable, or maybe the softer way the “er” trailed off the end that made his pronunciation of my name the most natural I'd ever heard. It was like my name was reborn in that moment. In a surprising way I began to feel like I belonged in Germany. That I would have fit in well with the thriving pre-Holocaust German-Jewish population of Berlin.

I felt compelled to explore the connection further. “Yes for six nights...and by the way, do you know what ‘Heltzer’ means? Like, what the translation is in English?”

He paused for a moment, his eyes searching for a way to explain. He began with a pantomime of someone running and out of breath, “...it is like, you are running, chasing after someone, always bothering, always rushing,” I arched my eyebrows but he didn't seem deterred. He continued, “You are someone who... annoys other people. I'm sorry my English is not so good, but this is Heltzen.”

“Heltzen? Or Heltzer?”

“Ah, Heltzer! That is right. No, I don't believe Heltzer has any meaning.”

*

This pretty well captured my week-long experience in Germany, at moments drawn in and at others alienated. I was at once curious to explore the dark contours of my people's history and yet tempted to reject the country outright, almost punish it, in the hope that it might tame a horrific past. Despite these conflicting sensations, I valued the Germany Close Up experience because it enabled me to come face-to-face with this troubled history while offering a realistic update on all that has happened since. In the end I was able to replace grainy black and white images of SS men with the living, breathing reality of modern Germany. I was able to hit the "refresh" button.

*

The "Aktion T4" Grey Bus Monument; the stark, white, empty shelves underground at Bebelplatz; the solemn pillars that populated the Monument to the Murdered Jews of Europe. Each site felt so unabashedly public, so visible. Somehow they'd transformed concrete, stone, and wood into vivid, visceral experiences. As my body swept through each I felt myself making the case to my ancestors: This was a country that wanted to face up to its past. It was not hiding, it was honest.

As the program moved from monuments, memorials, and memory to the forward-looking hopes, plans, and problem-solving of modern Germany I detected the same sense of sincere introspection. In our visit to a member of parliament I felt engaged with Germany's most pressing contemporary issues and challenges: What should our role be in European integration? How will we maintain leadership in export sectors? How will we integrate a growing immigrant population that feels isolated and estranged? I began to feel that in a way it was I who had been dishonest by summarizing a complex country and society into a 60-year-old generalization – one that wasn't reflective of a modern reality. My dominant impression of a hate-filled, power-hungry, morally bankrupt society began to recede – like bland pigments set in a rich and colorful mosaic that was beginning to take form. My prejudices were still present, but much less noticeable in my broader understanding of today's Germany.

It was at the Kreuzberg Initiative Against Antisemitism (KIgA) that I gained a real appreciation for the unique social challenges that Germany faces. It was a revelation that Germany itself was socially wounded after the war and that the scars still showed. At the KIgA session I learned about the experience of Turkish immigration to Germany and the problem of trying to imbue newcomers with a sense of patriotism and belonging when the lessons of misplaced nationalism were scattered across the country in plain sight. As an American and a Jew I had taken for granted my sense of belonging to these groups and the level of social cohesion woven together by shared experiences, language, and ritual. I began to think of the pledge of allegiance I recited each morning in grade school as an anomaly, and wondered how Germany would manage to introduce similar tools to prevent a destructive divergence in its society. If the American naturalization process ensures immigrants understand the principles upon which the country was founded, what could Germany point to as the bare bones essentials of being "German?" What was the glue that should hold the German people together?

Halfway through the trip, steeped in the emotional experience of confronting our past and initiating a cautious rapprochement, we sat down as a group to "debrief;" to collectively process the experience of the first few days.

Over various stimulants and depressants our group moved through the conversation organically, speaking from instinct and passion. It seemed that just as we updated our understanding and impressions of Germany we also reconnected with the question of where Jews have come as a people over the last 60 years, especially American Jews. We came from a wide range of backgrounds, from Reform to Orthodox, from spiritually engaged to defiantly disengaged, from Zionist to politically ambivalent. Regardless of background, coming into such close contact with the sites of the Shoah made each of us wonder about these contradictions and think existential thoughts.

Were we losing our identity, blending into an increasingly secular American culture? Was it enough to be "culturally" Jewish with limited theology, or would this only dilute us with each successive generation? The spirit of Jewish debate was alive: raised voices; points and counterpoints; nods of agreement from the less vocal sitting along the walls. An interesting paradox emerged: Germany as a symbol of both the destruction and creation of modern Jewish identity. While it was the site of a genocide that sought to erase Jews from the cultural map of the world, much of my generation's Jewish identity is anchored by the Holocaust and the establishment of the State of Israel, both events that are irrevocably linked to Germany. As the passage of time made it easier for my generation to reconnect with Germany, the same dynamic threatened to erode the influence of these watershed events that seemed to make us who we are. What would bind our children and grandchildren to their Jewish identity?

As we left that evening with big questions unanswered I reflected on how unlikely it would have been for that conversation among young Jews to take place in America. We had to come to Germany to pluck ourselves out of our routine, in order to see ourselves with a zoomed-out lens and grapple with broader issues that we rarely considered while preparing for final exams, an

The author together with fellow Germany Close Up participants and guide

upcoming promotion, or deciding where to eat on a Saturday night. Ironically, Germany presented itself as a "safe house," for us to confront our Judaism.

But just as I felt drawn closer to the country I took a step or two back. When we boarded the U-Bahn back to Mitte that evening we were joined by a group of skinheads clad in black leather, huddled around a group of seats in the middle of the train car. As my eyes moved over the tattoos on one man's knuckles I wondered if he could tell that I was Jewish. My body tensed as I observed others in our group, some visibly on alert and others unaware. In a brief moment the prejudices I had laid to rest in the preceding days came back to life. The introspection, honesty, and contrition that I had so admired now seemed less triumphant, the progress more precarious. The voices of my ancestors echoed: "Do not be fooled, we must always be suspicious, it was our false sense of comfort that led to catastrophe."

*

In writing this essay two years after the Germany Close Up program I've realized the trip was a truly transformative experience. It turned my dated and static impression of a country into a dynamic, nuanced, and ultimately more "real" relationship with a place inextricably linked to my people's past. I feel proud to have taken the opening to explore forgiveness and redemption, both for myself and for my ancestors who were also present for that week, in my character, in my heart, in my DNA. While the process left countless loose ends, I appreciated that it forced me to contemplate important new questions and think new thoughts.

When I think of Germany now, the grainy black and white images have come to life in a colorful and complex contemporary reality. I think of *schnell* and *achtung* in the context of history lessons and greet my newfound German friends with *wie geht's* and *krass*. As we march through the 21st century, I'm glad to be an American Jew who now knows Germany more for what it *is* than what it *was*, and to be able to convey a more grounded version of the country to my children and grandchildren in the generations to come.

Germany Up Close and Personal: History, Religion, and the Reinheitsgebot

Ira D. Glasser

"In less than 13 hours, I will be leaving for Newark Airport. Destination: Berlin."

These words mark the first line of the journal I recorded while on Germany Close Up and my subsequent travels throughout the country. Having spent a total of 24 days, visiting 15 different cities, and sampling 64 different types of beer in the summer of 2009, my experiences are constantly in mind and used professionally. Staying up to date with German news and using photos and experiences when teaching about Germany in my classroom are only a few examples. Almost two years later, I am still amazed at how much I saw of the country and learned from the people.

I think back to my discussions with peers and family about why I wanted to go to Germany and compare them to those that I have today about why I went and what was gained. Considering my expectations, recollections, and sensations, I listened to, rather than just heard, what Germany and the German people had to say. As an "immersed tourist," I wanted to experience Germany through three lenses: history, Judaism, and beer. The historical and Jewish lenses were easily related; the "beer" lens offered me the opportunity to explore various parts of these cities, engage and talk with local residents. These intertwined themes helped shape not only my relationship with Germany, but helped me reshape my Jewish identity.

Before Germany Close Up, my relationship with Germany was a growing yet subtle one. I never seriously thought about modern Germany, its people, and the impact the war had had on the generations of Germans since 1945. While studying for my Bachelor's degree, I enrolled in the course, *The Holocaust*. On the first day, what intrigued me most was that our professor was German and not Jewish. I wondered how he came to teach the Holocaust. When I asked him about his family history during office hours, he replied that I would have to wait until the end of the course to find out. Over the months, our relationship grew. At the end of the semester, he told me his family history: his grandfather, a veteran of World War I, was a member of the Nazi Party who tried to work his way up through its ranks; both of his parents were members of the Hitler Youth; another relative of his remained a staunch antisemite until his death. Instead of being angry or confused (as I had thought

I would be), I was more understanding of how historical circumstances and events mold people's lives. As a result, my relationship with Germany began.

This relationship remained dormant for a few years, until I enrolled in another course in graduate school. I was forced to confront German history as an academic, once again looked at German history objectively, and saw history as cause and effect, rather than isolated events, people, places, and ideas. During the semester and afterwards, a friend and I frequently debated about German history and our personal connection with Germany. Using the ideas from the class, I often took positions defending Germany (and its people) while considering a much larger picture; whereas she focused on specific events that usually countered my positions. We hypothesized why a German could support National Socialism in 1933. I often cited the Depression, a fragmented and failing democracy, and the betrayal of other European countries and the United States, as examples. Eventually, she went on Germany Close Up and when she came home the first thing she told me was, "You need to do this program."

I was not quite sure what to expect from Germany and Germany Close Up. I spoke with alumni (from whom I heard about the program) and knew what the program logistically entailed. I knew that we would meet with representatives from organizations such as the Kreuzberger Initiative gegen Antisemitismus and the Ministry of Foreign Affairs; visit historical sites such as the Ravensbrück concentration camp and the Berlin Wall Memorial. What I did not know, nor could I fathom, was where my observations, conversations, emotions, and thoughts would take me. There was no conceivable way for me to predict these. I prepared myself as much as possible by reading the materials that Germany Close Up sent, reviewed notes from German history classes that I took in graduate school, and read and learned about the sites and organizations I was going to visit. After this, all I could do was come up with questions, wonder, and be patient. Knowing I was going to travel outside of Berlin after the trip, a nervous pit sat in my stomach. I was rather unsure of what was on the horizon – whom would I meet and what would I experience? All I knew for sure was that this trip was necessary, especially at this point in my life.

History guided me throughout Berlin and Germany. Everywhere my feet and the U-Bahn took me had historical significance. At the end of my first day in Berlin, I recorded, "I think it is possible to experience and feel history in Berlin differently than any other place I have been so far..." It was difficult to ignore history in Berlin; the city was saturated in it. The architecture, the layout of the city, and the memorials walk you through more than 140 years of German, world, and Jewish history. One could visit the Brandenburger Tor, which could represent Napoleon's victory over the Prussian military, Napoleon's defeat, a center of Nazi marches, the post war division, or the reunification of Germany in 1989. The memorials are just as layered with meaning. The Memorial to the Murdered Jews of Europe, for example, placed between East and West Berlin near the Brandenburger Tor, is in close proximity to the former Gestapo headquarters in Berlin and Hitler's bunker. Additionally, it is purposely left open to individual interpretation, while memorializing the victims of Nazi persecution.

Jewish history and culture came alive in Berlin. As a group, we stayed in the Mitte neighborhood. Once the heart of Jewish Berlin, Mitte is home to the Neue Synagoge, a representation of the rich Jewish culture and life. It stands out from synagogues I have visited in Spain and the Czech Republic, as well as the synagogue I attend in New York City. Rather than blending in or being hidden in the architecture of the city, this synagogue stands out – in color, ornamentation, and size. We stayed near the former site of the Hochschule für die Wissenshaft des Judentums – one of the first institutions to promote the study of Judaism as a social science. I have not only learned about this in various courses of study for both my Bachelor's and Master's degrees, I have studied according to its philosophy, and have taught Jewish history, religion, and culture as a social science class rather than a course of religion.

Along with exploring highlights of Jewish history, we delved into learning about and discussing the Holocaust. The night before we visited the Ravensbrück concentration camp, I sat up thinking about what it was going to be like visiting a Nazi concentration camp for the first time. Images of other camps flashed through my memory. Feelings of reading *Night* and *Survival at Auschwitz* came back to me. This was the first time I had heard about Ravensbrück, and I wondered how it would be similar and different to photos and videos I had seen. I wondered how I would emotionally react. These questions continued to occupy my thoughts as we turned onto the unpaved road that led to the camp.

Initially, I had similar feelings as when I visited Yad Vashem in Jerusalem. All of a sudden, standing outside the crematorium, I became overwhelmed with sadness, anger, and confusion. I wondered how could the average German citizen claim not to have known what was happening? As I pondered this, I realized only in such a powerful police state as Nazi Germany could such a fear exist within the people that they would not want to speak up or against such atrocities. Still, questions loomed.

After the visit, we reflected and processed the experience as a group. People shared their thoughts, including our German guides. One shared her family history and how she has coped with it. She told us that she knew there that one of her grandparents was responsible for the deaths of innocent people. At the same time, she knew him as a loving grandfather. Then, she said something striking. For her, remembering and talking about history, including her family history was a decision she came to at a young age. She cannot feel personally responsible for the lives lost, yet at the same time feels that something must be done to honor the memories of the victims. This opened a floodgate of questions, thoughts, and feelings. Conflicted and unsettling emotions kept me awake that night.

The whirlwind of emotions that occupied me persisted throughout the remainder of the trip. I yearned for more organic and authentic experiences in Germany. I wanted to do what my German peers did. A few of us from Germany Close Up went to a screening of *Der Himmel über Berlin* in an open-air cinema. Our guides recommended we see the film, and we were among the only Americans in the small outdoor courtyard theater. Thankfully, the film had subtitles, and provided visual evidence of what East and West Berlin looked like two years before the Berlin Wall fell. As I watched the film, I tried to identify various places in Berlin and compare them to what I had seen in the past week.

Though the cinema was a starting point to experiencing German culture, some of the most memorable conversations and friendships were forged over beer – a pride of Germany. I processed my experiences and had open conversations with Germans young and old. At our dinner with German students, I befriended a student from Humboldt University, who opened his home to me for the two extra days I stayed in Berlin. While traveling to Nuremberg to visit the Dokumentationszentrum Reichsparteitagsgelände, a few German girls took me out to show me the nightlife. I am still in touch with them to this day, and saw them during a second visit to Germany last year. In Munich, an older German couple in town for the Munich Opera Festival sold me their extra ticket for *Lohengrin* by Richard Wagner. This was performed at the same opera house of its Munich premiere and had been sold out for five months. Moreover, I would not willingly have seen this opera if it were performed at the Metropolitan Opera. Two men I met at the Englischer Garten suggested I visit the Haus der Deutschen Kunst and see remnants of Nazi architecture that I did not find in my *Lonely Planet* tour book.

Inevitably I was asked, "What are you doing in Germany?" I explained that I was an American Jew and wanted to meet Germans, listen to what they had to say, and experience German culture differently from other tourists. I was here on Germany Close Up and that I wanted to incorporate history, Judaism, and beer into my experiences. Once I explained this, there was an urgency to address history immediately and not let it become the proverbial elephant in the room.

I began to appreciate the fact that as an American Jew, Germans and I were molded by the same history, albeit in profoundly different ways. My grandparents fought in World War II, my parents were born in the immediate post-war period, and we were an openly proud Jewish-American family who freely discussed the past. I never thought to consider how someone of my age in Germany approached the topic of the Holocaust and the war; Germans were a nameless, faceless enemy. I began this process thanks to my Holocaust professor, but it was not until I went to Germany and listened to their experiences that I started to understand – Jews and Germans of my generation share a similar past, though we share the burden differently.

As an educator, I value the importance of asking questions more than the answers themselves. I left Germany with a few answers; more significantly, however, I left with even more questions. Through Germany Close Up, I formed a deeper relationship with Germany and had the pleasure of returning a second time for an authentic German wedding. I continue to ask the same question, "What is my personal relationship with Germany?" but the question has since taken on a different meaning. Though the answer is constantly evolving, I have found that discussing history, Judaism, and beer, has allowed a seemingly foreign land become all too familiar.

Germany: Long Walls and Knitted Hens

Marc Keller

Germany Close Up was established in 2007 and brings young Jewish-Americans to experience modern Germany "up close and personally," as part of the country's effort to rebuild its relationship to world Jewry. I was excited about meeting the people and culture of today's Germany, but as I prepared for the trip, my expectations still largely revolved around the Holocaust and what it would be like to visit the actual site of Nazism. I wondered, too, what the attitude of modern Germans toward Jewish people would be, and whether there is an effort to deflect attention away from the Holocaust, in favor of more appealing aspects of Germany and German history.

It was not long, however, before I realized that it is quite the opposite. Discussing the Holocaust with the Germans we met, especially a group of Christian theology students, I sensed their sadness that their country is forever stained and that a part of their identity and national pride was stolen. And far from softening the atrocities, the historical sites and memorials in Germany have a harder edge and a more potent effect than any others I have seen. The sculpture of an overturned chair on Koppenplatz is a jarring memorial to the Jews who fled their homes or were kidnapped. The ground-flattener at Sachsenhausen, meant to be pulled by horses but forced upon human prisoners, has a sickening aura. And of course, taking up four acres of central Berlin, is the Memorial to the Murdered Jews of Europe, where, when asked about its grim name, our tour guide admonished us that "six million Jews did not *die* – they were murdered."

*

As I explored more of the city and its local color, however, the feeling I had had that my time in Germany would be dominated by grim reminders of Nazism was replaced by the realization that I was in *Berlin*, a major European city with an endless supply of everyday attractions. I had, of course, expected to find somber Holocaust memorials, like those mentioned above, which are part of the collective experience of Berlin, especially if the visitor is Jewish. But I did not quite expect to find a quirky, irresistible street musician playing a tableful of wineglasses. I did not quite expect to be so dazzled by the glow of Alexanderplatz at night. I did not expect to be so entertained by the small *DDR Museum* and its striking details of life in divided Germany, such as the Trabi car (and the years-long wait that people endured to receive one), and the proliferation of nude beaches in the GDR, as a last bastion of personal liberty. And I certainly did not expect to find the Brandenberg Gate's *Raum der Stille*, the Room of Silence, a small space of quiet repose in the center of a bustling city of three million people, providing an opportunity for everyone to remember the past, but also, as the Room's brochure mentions, to meditate and feel gratitude for the achievements of recent years.

*

Soon we were off to Oberammergau, to misty Alps and pastoral landscapes, and of course the fabled *Passionsspiele*, the Passion Play, one of the cornerstones of our trip. But around the play were other experiences and memories. There was our lunch with Mayor Nunn, our stroll through Oberammergau with Otto Huber, and our private tour of the playhouse with the director of the play, Christian Stückl, and his cigarette filled grin. But most memorable was my time with Irma, "house mother" to the four of us who stayed in her home. Irma, who had never met a Jewish person and yet was a perfect Jewish *bubbe*. Irma, who assured us that there was no pork on the breakfast table, and who of course served us the requisite European boiled egg, nestled in a knitted egg-warmer shaped like – what else – a hen.

It may seem peculiar that, in the whirl of activity surrounding the decennial Passion Play, a knitted hen is so memorable. But it is. I will never see Irma again – but so too will I never eat a boiled egg without recalling her knitted hens. And so, too, when I am reminded of the Holocaust, and am tempted to hate Germany or Germans, I can recall Irma. Irma, who was alive during World War II and the Nazi regime. But also Irma, who, in modern Germany, 2010, welcomed a group of Jews into her home, made sure not to serve pork, and bundled us in extra blankets for a chilly evening at the Passion Play.

*

If my time in Berlin was marked by Holocaust memorials, in Munich I experienced more of contemporary Jewish life in Germany, primarily at the Ohel Jakob Synagogue, which is part of the New Jewish Center complex. There is an impressive prayer area, and our group was privileged to dine at Restaurant Einstein, the elite kosher eatery adjoining the synagogue. But there is also a wall of names on the lower level of the synagogue, names of Munich Jews killed in the Holocaust, and the wall is horrifyingly long and dense. Accompanying the wall is a book, also horrifyingly long and dense, containing biographical and genealogical information on these victims.

"Kiss of Judas" scene from the Passion Play, Oberammergau

There is a name that is *not* on the wall, however, and that is that of Charlotte Knobloch, born in Munich, in 1932, to an affluent family and who survived the Holocaust as a young girl hiding with Catholic farmers in Bavaria. Today, she is a well-known leader of Munich's Jewish community, President of the Central Council of Jews in Germany, and one of the key forces behind the funding and construction of the New Jewish Center. She came to the synagogue to meet with our group in a small chapel room, and though I doubt any of us knew of her before that evening, I also doubt that any of us will ever forget her.

Hearing her story, in her own words and voice, was an unparalleled, utterly riveting experience – and that is an understatement. Here was a woman who, after the Holocaust, could have emigrated to America, or Israel, or anywhere else to get out of Germany – but who did the opposite and stayed, not only to rebuild Munich's Jewish community, but to foster reconciliation between modern Jewry and Germany. One of the stated intentions of Germany Close Up is to help Jews come to grips with the horrific Holocaust years, and there is no better model of this than Charlotte Knobloch, and for me, no better inspiration than our private time with her.

*

Beyond exploring Jewish Munich, my time in the city was dotted with small but memorable personal experiences. In Berlin I had eaten an asparagus dish at a restaurant, since this was the season and I like asparagus anyway, though I was more accustomed to the skinnier green stalks one usually sees in the States. In Munich everywhere there were vendors hawking the fat white asparagus, and the stalls seemed quaint and whimsical to me, perhaps because I had never seen quite so much attention paid to one vegetable.

There was also my afternoon at the *Neue Pinakothek*, one of Munich's premier art museums, which houses Edvard Munch's *Street in the Village of Aasgardstrand* (1902). It is always difficult to know, let alone explain, why a certain painting arrests one's attention so fully and intensely, but for several moments I stood frozen in the gallery, wholly absorbed in the pink swirl of Munch's enigmatic style.

But what does Munch and his picture of Aasgardstrand have to do with Munich's Jewish community, or its horrific past? Nothing, really. That is the point. Seventy years ago, as a Jew, I would not have had the opportunity to be mesmerized by a painting in a museum in Munich. But today, my religion and nationality made no difference whatsoever. I was simply a visitor to the museum, and appreciating that distinction between World War II-era Germany and modern Germany was a step toward genuine reconciliation.

Then it was my final evening in Munich, and Germany, and on my way back to the hotel I stopped in a snack shop. A candy aficionado, I had become quite familiar with the local offerings, but I did not expect the absolute *wall* of Haribo gummy candy that the store featured. When I finally dumped my bounty on the shopkeeper's counter, I made a fast friend, who joked with me and pointed out some choice varieties I had missed. During these moments I was not contemplating the Holocaust, not envisioning scenes of the pitch-black brutality of Nazism – not even shaking my head at the allegations that the Haribo Company used forced labor during World War II. I was simply in Munich, a dazzling world city and the epicenter of the Haribo gummy world. It was *fun* – pure *fun*, and trivial and childish as it may sound, that wall of gummy candy created another personal bond to Munich, and helped to make it *my* city, when, seventy years ago, it would have been anything but.

*

Shortly after returning home from Germany, I rewatched Roman Polanski's Holocaust film, *The Pianist.* As had happened upon my first viewing, years ago, I found myself scowling, glaring, my heart pounding. I wanted all of Germany to be forced to watch the film. I wanted to grind their noses into the screen. But then I remembered Irma and the knitted hen in Oberammergau. The *Raum der Stille* and Alexanderplatz at night in Berlin. Asparagus vendors and Munch's pink swirl in Munich. I remembered these things and I remembered Germany, *today*. I remembered where I had stared at the ground-flattener at Sachsenhausen – and where I had stared at a Berlin street musician playing a tableful of wineglasses. Where I had stood in front of a wall of murdered Jews in the basement of the Munich synagogue – and also where I had stood in front of a wall of Haribo gummy candy.

I am very fortunate to have had such a generous and well-planned opportunity, through the Germany Close Up program, to find and experience my private Germany. Not every Jewish person does, or will, or even wants one, and that is understandable and forgivable. My recollections are not meant to be flippant, or to make light of the Holocaust in any way or degree. We must not ever forget yesterday's atrocities, in part to ensure there are none tomorrow. Yet between yesterday and tomorrow is *today*, and today is not the Holocaust. While traveling through Berlin, Oberammergau, and Munich, I took it as my privilege and my responsibility to represent modern Jewry and to experience *modern* Germany – not to wallow in or nurture my hatred for Nazi Germany. And as I collected unexpected memories, images, and friends, I became part of a Jewish peoplehood that remembers yesterday without being enslaved by it, and that embraces progress and reconciliation, *today*.

Walking Far from Home

Marissa Kaplan

Just like reading *The Waves* by Virginia Woolf calls to mind the iridescent rhythm of Beethoven's late quartets because she listened to them incessantly throughout her writing of the novel, I can hardly separate my impressions of Germany from the music I had flowing into my ears during my time there. Every imprint, sensation, and mark that I took away from Germany can easily be recollected through the first song I listened to when I landed; the same one I had on repeat throughout my visit. Memories are entirely subjective matter, shaped by each person in his or her own way. Therefore, I know all that I was expecting and everything I got in return are reflective of me and my personal state of affairs at the time of my visit.

It would not have been difficult for a stranger to figure out what I was going through when I stepped onto the plane in Tel Aviv last summer on my way to Berlin. I'm sure my neighboring passenger heard through my low quality headphones just what I was hearing – moody, solemn tunes mimicking the heartache I was going through after suffering a personal breakup. Germany was only meant to be a bit of an escape from Tel Aviv. But it wound up being much more.

That is not to say I had no other thoughts of Germany, of course. It is critical, however, to understand that I am an American who had lost some of her patriotism and found her way to Israel about six years earlier. Israel, at the time of my move, spoke to a certain part of my identity as a Jew. But all the idealism that took me to Tel Aviv has imploded over the years. Israel turned out to be no more moral or conscientious a country than where I had come from. So, in my excitement to get to Germany, my open-mind and critical eye were both fully charged.

Germany Close Up had granted me the gift of being able to visit the country, but I was prepared to be hesitant about swallowing all that was fed to me on the trip. I was not sure of the precise agenda, but I was primed for being provided with a lot of one-sided and positive information, the validity of which I would have to assess in my own time. Germany is home to many of the philosophers and ways of thinking that I revel in and I knew that it had matured beyond its modern dark history to become a leader in the international realms of economics, politics, and social reform. Yet, my instant skepticism kept me from taking it all at face value.

Unfortunately, the Germany that is imprinted on too many of both my peers' and family members' minds is the one that stole lives and turned the world on its head only 70-somewhat-years-ago. It is hard to comprehend how an entire nation can allow what happened to happen. But I see it with my own eyes every day living Tel Aviv. I feel it in myself when I wake up some mornings; it's this dull nag in my brain that melts away during the day but that I am conscious of all the same. It is remarkable how powerful misinformation, veiled eyes, and potent slogans can be. They have the ability to take an entire society to the edge without them even knowing. It is easier to lie to ourselves than we all think.

As an individual, I was already past placing blame on Germany and Germans for World War II. But, I still did not know what to expect of the people. The only Germans I had ever met were colleagues of my father who always approached us with apologies for the Holocaust that I found embarrassing and unnecessary. I was well aware that they had not committed any crimes themselves. And my family was lucky enough not to have had any direct losses in World War II. The guilt that they carried on their shoulders was surely better than self-righteousness, but it was still misplaced. It was an uncalled for burden that weighed them down and made me red in the face.

The first thing that made my face burn on arrival, dragging my suitcase down the street in Berlin looking for my hotel, was a woman in sky-high platform boots wearing a revealing skirt and top that showed off her assets. I was stunned by how freely a woman in the center of town could dress and market herself to others. Her occupation is usually something that is frowned upon in most of the modern world and here she stood proudly showing herself off. When the blood finally drained from my face, I was struck with the first smile I remembered consciously in months. This is Germany: the unmentionable in your face and it's all right.

I quickly found my room and grabbed a few essentials to wander the streets that same evening. The group was not due to convene until the next afternoon, so I went out. The beat of "Walking Far From Home" by Iron and Wine was my soundtrack as I skipped along the streets that dewy night. I met up with some fellow travelers and danced salsa at the Tacheles building. It was a vibrant night that set the tone of the trip.

In the morning I woke up to go on a bike tour of Berlin. With the same song playing in the background, I relished the time I spent seeing the city both up close and breezing by on my bicycle. "I saw sunlight on the water/Saw a bird fall like a hammer from the sky/Saw an old woman on the speed train/She was closing her eyes," sang in my ears and similarly materialized before my eyes.[1] A small dose of history and architecture filled me up enough to last until the afternoon when I met up with my fellow participants of Germany Close Up.

It was easy to fall instantly in love with a city that combines so many things of the East and the West. That is what makes Berlin so dynamic to me; it is entirely modern, but also in transition, and with essential parts of its emergence deeply rooted in its history and turmoil. So much is controversial in Berlin's development, from changes in architecture due to reunification, the numerous memorials for commemoration, or the converging cultures and nationalities; what makes it interesting is that all this is current conversation. It is not a jaded city, quite the opposite; it is alive in all its diversity and problems.

In the evening, I met up with the other Americans joining me on the Germany Close Up program. I was excited to meet my peers and learn the reasons why they had set out to get to know Germany. Surrounding me were some of the most successful and talented young individuals whom I have ever been in the presence of or been included in a group with. Many people were the grandchildren of Holocaust survivors, coming to try to reconnect with a family history that had been altered at German hands. In my opinion, they were less on a mission to understand Germany today and more on a trip to absolve a family record of blame. It was obvious to me already that a great majority of those accompanying me would not be as driven to discover the intricacies of Germany, but were going to concentrate on their individual victimhood and how Germany had played and still plays a role in their misfortune.

Germany Close Up found a way to incorporate many of the different issues facing Germany today: from trying to incorporate a growing immigrant population, through assuaging its own guilt for past misdeeds, to becoming a leading global economic power and its relations with a dynamic international environment; we covered it all. Due to the questions and concerns of my peers, I found that our guests and speakers were often drowned with criticism of German relations with Iran, disapproval of Germany's reactions to Israel, and denigration of whether Germany is sensitive to a myriad of Jewish issues. I felt my cohorts held an unfair bias against Germany that they would never entirely concede.

1 *Iron and Wine, Walking Far From Home (Burbank, California: Warner Bros. Records, 2011), http://www.youtube.com/watch?v=o6vA3Z42Vz8.*

All this censure was displeasing; I did not fully grasp how they could walk so self-righteously. It was as if they were looking for some sort of formal apology or guilt stricken country to fess up. Germany had gotten up off its knees a long time ago, and was all the better because of it. One night, towards the end of our ten-day trip, I sat up trying to put to words what irked me so much about this reaction I sensed from my fellow participants. Also, why wasn't I more angry and attempting to find culpability in Germany?

I sat up and cracked open my laptop to blog a bit and let off some steam. I plugged in my headphones and listened to the lyrics...

I saw rain clouds, little babies
And a bridge that had tumbled to the ground
I saw sinners making music
I've dreamt of that sound, dreamt of that sound
I was walking far from home
But I carried your letters all the while
I saw lovers in a window
Whisper, "Want me like time, want me like time"
I saw sickness, blooming fruit trees
I saw blood and a bit of it was mine[2]

It hit me just then: for me, Germany is an inspiration. I had seen and witnessed so many people and parts of Germany thus far: everyday citizens, politicians making influential decisions, and journalists setting public opinion. They all came together to create a unique space in the middle of Europe. There are several other liberal and free-thinking countries that are easy to name, but they are not nearly as impressive as Germany because they have not had to overcome and rediscover so much and in such a short span of time.

There is very little you can take for granted in Germany. If its leaders and its people had not taken such specific and enormous steps in education, social improvement, and freedom of ideas, it would not be the same place today. From a society that once closed its eyes to evils that were bred on its own ground, generations of Germans have moved past guilt and shame to fully comprehend their responsibility to not let history repeat itself. Apologies are empty, but seeing a country that has made conscious amendments so that my generation in Germany now holds their heads up high and reflects on their world judiciously, well, that makes me smile all over again.

2 *Iron and Wine, Walking Far From Home.*

Yet, it is not just what Germany has become in and of itself that I find so rousing. Many countries in this world live in self-inflicted turmoil. Maybe the places I have lived will have the confidence and desire to make the dire changes I believe are necessary for continued existence. Though, not everyone is ready for the deep reflection and self-criticism I believe Germans have taken on over the last few generations. Still, knowing that it is possible, and that Germany is an example of a troubled society that was able to reenvision itself, brings back some of the optimism and confidence I have lost.

The Germany I was lucky enough to meet was mostly shown to me by the Germans with whom I came into contact. And while they are only a few minor individuals, they are enough to support my feelings about Germany. In some ways Germany is emblematic of its stigmas: you can see the exactness in the way buses arrive punctually or the primness in the formality of "Sie." But you only see the dynamics, the thinking, and the transformation that is Germany through the people. For that is what sums up any place, the people who compose it, the rhythm to which they walk, the tempo of their hearts,and the harmony of their thoughts.

The author with fellow Germany Close Up participants

My Own Private Germany

Erin Levi

I inhaled a slight breath – a habit developed from extensive living in polluted environments. The air, however, was forest-like and crisp: unexpectedly fresh for a capital city at the height of summer. Straight off the plane and onto the city bus, this was my first impression of Berlin. I savored another breath, much deeper this time, and felt cleansed from the stresses of travel as I exhaled. I relayed my observation to my Aunt Ingrid, who had come from Iserlohn, a small town several hours away, to greet me at Berlin-Tegel International Airport. "Ah, *ja*, the *Berliner Luft*," she noted in a charming Teutonic accent. "*Luft* means air?" I guessed, having had no German language education. "*Ja*, it is quite famous, too," she added. "In fact, my elderly neighbor asked me to bring him back a bag of *Berliner Luft* when I return! And, you know, there is even a song about it." She began to sing unreservedly, welcoming a bus of new arrivals with a playful tune:

Das macht die Berliner Luft
Luft
Luft

so mit ihrem holden Duft
Duft
Duft

wo nur selten was verpufft
pufft
pufft

A city that has a song about its clean air – could this be true? As a New Yorker, this was hard to believe. When finished with her short serenade, to which she bounced her knees in tempo, Aunt Ingrid explained that the air comes in fresh from the Baltic Sea, which borders the northern side of the country, keeping the climate temperate. Looking out the window, I observed an abundance of trees, parks, and cycling denizens; I couldn't help but think that nature and eco-friendly Berliners were equally responsible for this song-inspiring *Luft*.

"I'm so happy you are here, finally!" Aunt Ingrid gleamed with excitement. "I cannot wait to show you my Berlin where I grew up." It's true, I had promised her for years I would come to visit, but for various reasons never was able to – from parents who weren't "keen" on travel to Germany, to say the least, to not having the money or reason to go myself. Now with my acceptance on a trip sponsored by Germany Close Up in affiliation with the American Jewish Committee, I not only had an occasion, but I would also be there just two months before her 75th birthday. It was the perfect time indeed. The plan was to spend a couple of days with my Aunt sightseeing around Berlin, take a day trip to the medieval Baltic port town of Wismar to visit her children – my cousins – whom I had not seen in over twenty years, and then I'd move on to the purpose of my trip: a 10-day educational program for American Jews, like me, to "meet Modern Germany" through an immersion in Berlin life and society, with the chance to meet and engage with a range of people, from high level government officials to academics, minority groups, Israelis living in Berlin, and "young Germans."

Although I had been to Germany twice before – once when my grandfather was still living to visit Mühringen, the town in the Black Forest in which he grew up, and another time to visit my Aunt in Iserlohn, during a semester I spent in Milan, Italy, I was looking forward to reconnecting and learning more about a country in which my paternal family has deep roots (a family tree shows that my German heritage dates back to at least the 17th century). A country, which for most of my life growing up, I was discouraged to explore with fair reason. I could speak multiple languages, from Italian to Spanish, French, Vietnamese, and *even* Uzbek, but knew not more than a few words of German, as it was the one language my parents would not support me in learning. To them, it was still the language of the Nazis. So given the opportunity to rebuild a relationship with a country, which would have been my home had the course of history been different and kinder, I accepted.

As soon as we had arrived and settled into our artsy hotel in Mitte, Aunt Ingrid and I were off to have lunch at her favorite place in Berlin: the Hackesche Höfe. She first gave me a tour of the courtyards, all beautifully renovated except for one, which was left overgrown with ivy. It was kept in its original condition to act as a memorial to the Holocaust. Even on day one, there was no escaping these reminders of Germany's horrific past. After wandering around and contemplating the difficult history of the streets we walked, we made our way back to a beautiful open courtyard to have lunch outside at a restaurant called "Oxymoron," which felt like a gamble considering its name. While waiting for our food, we enjoyed sounds of birds chirping (the space was surprisingly free of any urban noises) and observed streams of light cascading down the blue and cream ceramic tiles of the buildings around us, which were built in *Jugendstil*. Finally our lunch was served: a filet of fish pan-fried with a thinly grated golden-brown potato crust, served atop sliced cabbage in a very light cream sauce and garnished with a sprig of tarragon. I took one bite and thought I could not be happier; who were all of those critics of German cuisine? Surely they had not tried this!

Looking across the table into Aunt Ingrid's chestnut-hued owl-shaped eyes, I felt like I was looking into the eyes of my grandfather, *Opa*, who had escaped Nazi Germany in 1937. Why Ingrid is still in Germany and the rest of my family is not is a story of cinematic proportions. In essence, Ingrid was the illicit lovechild of my grandfather, whose name was Berthold, and his paramour, Erna, a Christian woman; illicit because in 1935, as a result of the Nuremberg race laws, it was illegal for a Jew to marry a non-Jew. With the Gestapo aware of the affair, the situation became too dangerous to continue and so in 1937, two years after the birth of their daughter Ingrid, Opa escaped to Holland and eventually went on to the United States, where he joined the U.S. Army and conducted interrogations for the Army's Intelligence – ironically, encountering a former "friend" of his from Mühringen who had put my Opa's father into *Dachau*. With extreme fortune, my great grandfather was able to get out after six weeks (and later emigrate to the U.S.) because he had won the Iron Cross in World War I and had received help from the Baron of his village. Opa eventually married Charlotte Stern, a German Jew from Wiesbaden who moved to New York City in 1933, and had my father Bruce, an only child, or so my father thought, until the age of 32 when he learned he had a half-sister in Germany named Ingrid.

I heard more about this story from Aunt Ingrid the next day, during a four-hour architectural boat tour of Berlin. Over the grassy banks of the river Spree, where people sat relaxing in lounge chairs, reading, sunning, and drinking, Ingrid pointed to a sign, which read "Charlottenburg," and said, "That is where I used to live." Her former neighborhood looked quite elegant and old compared to the newer and modern parts of Berlin. There, Ingrid grew up never knowing who her real father was until the year 1980 at age 45, when she had a family of her own. She told me she found out "by accident" from her mother's boss, Walter, when he slipped, "The older you get, the more you look like your father." Her complexion was olive, with brown hair and eyes just like Opa's; she didn't look like a "typical German." Ingrid told me, "I had always believed my father was living in East Germany, because my mother felt it was too dangerous for me to know that I was half Jewish."

Ingrid asked Walter who her real father was, but as he was sworn to secrecy, he apologized that her mother had not told her anything and said that all he could reveal was that he lived in the United States and "is a wonderful man."

"Right away, I went to my mother and demanded the truth," Ingrid explained. "And there, on the kitchen table, was an Easter card from your Opa to my mother that had arrived earlier that day. He had been thinking of us for months, so he wrote." (Ingrid, although half-Jewish, was raised a Catholic.) She took this as an auspicious sign for her to get in touch with him, so when she finally did speak with him on the phone, she said "We understood each other immediately." Without any hesitation, he welcomed her into our family. The unconventionality of the situation brought some dissent from certain relatives initially, relayed Ingrid, but luckily for me, I grew up knowing her as my Aunt.

To be able to spend time with my Aunt in Germany – sightseeing, storytelling – was very precious to me. Being with her brought to life the after-effects of the Holocaust and my sole, living connection to Germany. And so, with the start of my Germany Close Up program, I felt fortunate to have already experienced something special, something that I could call my own. But I also knew that my experience belonged in a collective context as well, and was looking forward to building new memories of Germany with people whom I hoped would become my friends.

When I arrived in the lobby of the Hotel Augustinenhof, coincidentally a few minutes walk from the Hackesche Höfe, I met a group of students and young professionals who immediately struck me as very bright, engaging, and warm. There was a level of uneasiness in the room, however, as we knew that this trip was certainly not a vacation and would be emotionally and intellectually challenging at times. When we went around introducing ourselves and explaining why we had chosen to participate, I learned, much to my surprise, that I was the only one who had a living connection to Germany. Many of the other participants might have had German heritage or European grandparents who had been in concentration camps; others had no direct connection at all, as their heritage was Sephardic, like Yaron, who was of Persian and Afghan descent.

I learned more about Yaron's interesting heritage over dinner at *Max und Moritz* with the "Young Germans." Yaron and I sat across from a rather reserved, bespectacled computer engineer named Dirk, whose knowledge of his own family's history was a bit fuzzy. Like other Germans we had met, he said that his grandparents were too young to have been involved. When we prodded further, he said he believed his great grandmother was Jewish and married an SS officer in London, because they were in love. The conversation did not have anywhere to go, and Dirk was still quiet and closed. I asked if he knew the song, *"Hoppe hoppe Reiter,"* which Opa would sing to me as a child, dipping me off his knee at the end each time. Immediately, Dirk perked up and sang the rest of the lyrics, saying he heard it as a child and was dipped at the end, too. Conversation then shifted to language – we asked Dirk how Germans say, "Hey dude, what's up?" and for the remainder of the evening we were practicing, *"Na Meister, alles klar?"* hopelessly messing up the inflection, which made Dirk laugh. We enjoyed a flaming *Flammkuchen* for dessert, and then we consulted him on where to go out at night: after listing a variety of clubs which featured "the best electronic music," Dirk told us about the "Beer Mile" on Karl Marx Allee – an international beer festival. Yaron and I were excited – not just about the beer festival, but about the fact that we had finally connected with Dirk.

Talk of family history can be an awkward and difficult topic, but over the years in Germany, it has become more common, with younger generations of Germans wanting to learn and come to terms with their past, like our Germany Close Up guide, Lena, who told us very poignantly about how she wanted to know the truth behind her family's involvement during World War II, and decided one day to confront her grandparents. I imagined what bravery this would take, and felt both indebted and connected to Lena. I had always looked at the Holocaust from the point of view of a survivor; never had I thought what it would be like to be the descendent of a perpetrator, and the burden of history and shame that that person would have to carry, not to mention, the responsibility.

It was thus understandable that time was needed for Germans to process the horrors of the Holocaust so that they would never be repeated again. As one of our speakers explained, "German memory of the Holocaust functions the opposite of human memory; the more time that passes, the more Germany remembers," pointing out the Holocaust Memorial, which was not unveiled until 2005 upon the 60th anniversary of the end of World War II, as an example.

Berlin, which was largely destroyed in the war, has rebuilt itself in a modern, fresh way. Yet, at the same time, its history has not been erased, on the con-

Participants of the Germany Close Up student program in affiliation with the American Jewish Committee's ACCESS program, August, 2010

trary, it has been purposely incorporated, with engraved brass cobble stones on streets marking the houses where Jews once lived, to double cobble stone lines showing where the Wall once was, and grassy areas that have been protected because underneath them lies a Jewish cemetery that was destroyed. Empty spaces, but spaces of history and memory.

I was surprised to learn that much of the remembrance is driven by non-Jews, from Germans who have chosen Jewish Studies as their major at university, to those who become tour guides at the Jewish Museum Berlin, concentration camps (like Sachsenhausen, which we visited), and the Holocaust Memorial; and those who have been (and are) supportive of Israel, working on kibbutzim and learning Hebrew. These are efforts that mean something to someone whose great grandparents were in a concentration camp, whose grandparents escaped to start a new life in America, whose parents did not want her to study German in school or visit the country on an exchange program when she was younger.

Six weeks after returning to New York, the same week in which I had the fortune to meet Chancellor Merkel at the Leo Baeck Institute where she was being honored (a perk of being an alumnus of Germany Close Up), I was invited by the Chabad in my apartment building in Williamsburg to celebrate the Jewish holiday of *Sukkot* on our rooftop. As soon as I arrived, it began to thunderstorm. The thatched roof typical of a *Sukka* did little to prevent the rain from getting in. As we watched our plates of food collect droplets of water, one man tried to stay dry by wearing a closed umbrella atop his head as a hat, with the handle comically dangling by his chin. And then, the power went out. I decided to take the opportunity to get to know the people seated next to me, as the service was seemingly interrupted. I detected a familiar accent from the man to my left and asked him where he was from. "Germany," he said, "from Berlin."

"I was just in Berlin over the summer! I loved it. And I met your Chancellor this week!"

Then I asked if he was Jewish and he said yes. I asked him to specify what kind of Jew and he confirmed, "I'm a German Jew." I could not believe it: after spending two weeks in Germany where I essentially met no "German Jews" (we met others: Israelis, Russian Jews, and expatriates), who would have thought I would meet a real German Jew on the rooftop of my building in Williamsburg, Brooklyn? We talked about how he was trying to get back in touch with his Jewish roots – his grandfather never left Germany after surviving Dachau and subsequently raised his family without any religion – as well as his reason for being in town: to photograph New York's diverse Jewish community. Because he was a photographer, we discussed Berlin's cutting edge art scene, and I asked him if he had seen The Boros Collection, which was one of the highlights of my program.

Then, the girl sitting to my right who was overhearing our conversation asked if I had been on Germany Close Up. "Why yes," I told her, and as it turned out, so had she the year before, and she even knew my program guide, Uli Schäfer, whose friend from Berlin would be staying at my apartment that coming weekend. If I had picked a different seat, I thought, the night would not have been so memorable or mind-blowing.

It was then that I realized that Germany for me was no longer just a place in history or a country on a map, but a living experience that I carry wherever I am, connecting me unexpectedly to many wonderful people. I feel lucky to have been given the chance to be on Germany Close Up, and eagerly await future life-enriching moments – in Germany, or elsewhere.

From Berlin to Yerushalayim

Eryn Schultz

When I stumbled upon the Maybachufer Wochenmarkt, I was prejudiced against her from the start. The name hardly rolls off the Anglicized tongue. Predictably, it clove to my mouth like a gob of crunchy, dry peanut butter. However, my prejudice would not last long. Within a few moments of arriving, the smell of piping-hot morsels of spinach and feta cheese wrapped in savory phyllo dough had won me over. While my mouth concentrated on phyllo pastry, my eyes took in the scene around me. Women in head scarves juggling children and make-shift shopping carts filled the scene. They weaved dangerously close to the vendors hawking their wares from the stalls that lined one main street in Kreuzberg. Picturesque grapes, strawberries, and peaches vied for my attention against a background of homemade breads, cheeses, and pastries.

Slowly, I tried to reconcile images of doner kebab and pita with my initial vaguely formed impressions of Germany. Yet, the very essence of the market seemed to rebuff the country's reputation for excessive order, cleanliness, and civility and validate an edgier, less tidy image of the nation. The rest of my experiences in Germany only furthered my confusion. When the time on the bus schedule exactly predicted the arrival of the bus and the people on the street approached me, an obviously lost tourist, with offers of help and directions, it was easy to default to a neat, homogeneous vision of Deutschland. However, it was always in these moments that Germany would reveal one of her many contradictions: the austere concrete blocks of the East Berlin library and the lyric classicalism of her West Berlin counterpart; the traditional old-world vibe of an outdoor, Turkish market and the overwhelming modernity of Potsdamer Platz and the Hauptbahnhof; a nation guilty of the crimes of the Holocaust and home to Europe's third-largest and fastest growing Jewish community.[1]

As a young American Jew wandering the streets of Berlin, it was this final contradiction that fascinated me. How could the country that birthed the Third Reich possibly play host to a modern Jewish community? The streets offered few answers to my question. Headscarves and other trappings of Islam could be seen in abundance, but kippot and obvious signs of Judaism were notably absent. On Dr. Pruin's tour of Berlin, I realized the presence of the

1 *"Latkes and vodka: Immigrants from the former Soviet Union are transforming Jewish Life in Germany," The Economist, January 3, 2008.*

Jewish community rested all around me: I just had to look down. On street corners throughout the city, raised cobblestones inscribed with names, birth dates, and the place of death, marked the homes and residences where Berlin's lost Jews once lived. Called "stumbling stones," these simple memorials were designed to introduce Holocaust remembrance into the mundane. As individuals literally stumbled upon these uneven bits of pavement on their way to work, school, and home, they would be forced to contemplate the legacy of the Final Solution. However, this sort of Jewish "presence" was not what I was looking for. I knew about Germany's connection to the Holocaust, but the country claimed to host a vibrant and active community today. Where was it?

Germany Close Up program director, Dagmar Pruin, at the "Block of Women" sculpture ensemble at Berlin's Rosenstraße memorial guiding participants on her walking tour "Empty Space? Don't Trust the Green Grass!"

Unfortunately, I did not find the Jewish community on the streets of Berlin. I never saw an errant Magen David peeking out from a shirt collar; no echoes of Yiddish drifted to me across subway cars. In fairness, I would be hard pressed to find outward signs of the Jewish community in any major city in the United States outside of New York. Nevertheless, as Berlin proved, something does not need to be obvious to exist. When I crossed through from the outside into community centers, synagogues, and kosher restaurants, I found the Jewish Germany. It is not the Jewish community of yesteryear; nor, is it the Jewish community of the United States. Instead, the Jewish community of Berlin has morphed and changed into something utterly distinct and uniquely German. While the population is oft heralded as "Europe's third-largest and fastest growing" Jewish community, immigration from the Soviet Union, not internal growth, has fueled the population surge. Over 70% of modern German Jews have Soviet heritage.[2] Many of these Jews were deemed Jewish not by their maternal heritage – as prescribed in Halacha, Jewish Law – but rather by the classification system institutionalized by the Soviet Union. These Soviet Jews enter with their own interpretation of Modern Judaism – one that often bears little resemblance to Judaism's traditional teachings and practices.[3]

Thus, while we Jews grow in population numbers, the Jewish traditions and institutions of Germany are in a state of flux. When my Germany Close Up group met with the head of the Centrum Judaicum, he spoke about the challenge of maintaining the traditional German-Ashkenazi character of the Jewish community while integrating the new, Soviet members without whom the entire German-Jewish community would have died out. Similar questions of identity and change gripped the Jewish community at the end of World War II when survivors of the war chose either to stay in or to return to Germany. Those who decided to continue their lives in Germany faced many questions of how to rebuild and move on from the past while adequately remembering and commemorating their lost loved ones. This struggle has joined with modern questions of who is a Jew and what this entails in forming the German-Jewish community today.

Perhaps, no one site better embodies the dual themes of change and renewal than the Old-New Synagogue. The golden dome of this iconic Jewish landmark glitters from a distance and brazenly asserts the continuation of Jewish life in the very heart of Berlin. While the original main sanctuary is a museum and no longer a functional house of worship, the group of Jews who gather in this holy place every Saturday morning continue the traditions of the German Jews of old. Like their German ancestors, some of the first Jews to espouse modernizing traditional Judaism, they are not Orthodox Jews in the most conventional sense. When I had the pleasure of attending Shabbat services, the female leader led the davening clothed in Talit.[4] Despite these deviations from the past, the service embodied the time-old values and practices of Shabbat as they have been enacted for centuries. Despite Hitler and Eichmann and Buchenwald and Wannsee, Germany's Jews have retooled and rebuilt. We Jews are *survivors* of anything the world can throw at us.

2 *"Latkes and vodka: Immigrants from the former Soviet Union are transforming Jewish Life in Germany," The Economist, January 3, 2008.*

3 *Jeffery Peck, Being Jewish in the New Germany (New Brunswick; New Jersey; London: Rutgers University Press, 2006), 111.*

4 *A Jewish prayer shawl traditionally worn exclusively by men.*

This message of survival was only reinforced when I left Germany. Unlike most members of my trip, my Germany Close Up experience was not a ten-day sojourn away from the United States. My trip was the first leg on a seven-month journey whose primary destination was Israel. Thus, when I stepped off the plane from Berlin, I transitioned not back into the United States, but into Eretz Yisrael. As I prepared to traverse the geographic divide separating Germany and Israel, I couldn't help but reflect upon the strong, metaphysical bond connecting Germany and Israel – the country, which tried to wipe out the Jewish people and the state that originated out of a global community's guilt for their silence.

Ironically, my arrival in Israel coincided with Tisha B'Av – the anniversary of the destruction of both the First and the Second Temples. The memorial holiday is one of the six fast days observed in Judaism, and an event of which I had remained ignorant until my Germany Close Up trip; the holiday had not made its way into my childhood Hebrew school education. However, the three Orthodox members of my Germany Close Up trip all maintained traditional observance of Tisha B'Av. When they were unable to attend a performance of the German Opera, I was confused. I was unaware of any situation, other than Shabbat, in which religion limited us Jews, a people of culture, from enjoying a work of art. However, as I learned, for the three weeks leading up to the holiday, the entire Jewish people are supposed to mimic a state of mourning. During this period, no celebrations should be scheduled; no live music should be heard. The seven days immediately before the holiday involve an even stricter level of self-denial. Luxuries, such as meat, are forbidden, and a somber tone grips the Jewish nation. When I realized I would have the privilege of being in Israel on the day of the destruction of my people's most holy of sites, I committed myself to finding a way to get to Jerusalem and the Western Wall.

A power on high truly must have orchestrated my attendance at the Cotel on Tisha B'Av because just days before my flight to Israel, I received an unsolicited invitation to visit Jerusalem the morning after my arrival in Eretz Yisrael. The cousin of the family friend I was staying with had made plans to visit Yad Vashem, Israel's Holocaust Museum, on Tisha B'Av, and she had room in her car. Riding this precipitous chain of events, my first morning in Israel I dressed carefully. I donned a long-sleeved shirt and floor-length skirt despite the 40°C heat. I drank no water and ate no breakfast. For the first time in my life, I prepared to observe Tisha B'Av as a traditional Jew.

At my first stop of the day, I found myself at yet another Holocaust memorial – Yad Vashem. However, this time I found myself in the land of the victims and not the perpetrators of the Shoah. When I arrived in Israel, surrounded by the children and relatives of Holocaust survivors, I could experience a Holocaust memorial knowing that almost everyone around me lived in active defiance of Hitler's dream. Emotionally drained, fatigued by fast, I transitioned from paying homage to the survivors of the Holocaust to mourning the destruction of the First and Second Temples. As I stood in front of the Cotel, the Western Wall of the Second Temple, sweltering in the heat, woozy from the lack of water and food, my heart swelled with pride. Not only did I feel proud to be in Jerusalem, standing at the last remnant of the Second Temple, lamenting the loss of Judaism's most holy site, but I also felt proud to be a Jew. I contemplated the centuries of oppression visited upon my people, the Spanish Inquisition, the Russian Pogroms, the Babylonian exile, the German Holocaust, and I was honored to inherit such a stubborn and tenacious history. Israelis call themselves Sabras after the spiny and resilient cactus plants that thrive in the hot desert. I find the name appropriate for the modern staff bearers of the Jewish people.

My decision to go to Israel for six months derived from my desire to finally figure out what it means to be Jewish and what it means to be Zionist. As a leftist, a feminist, and an American as well, could I really reconcile all five of these identity tags? Germany was not originally intended to play a part in this journey. I received the email advertising the program's July-August trip in late May in the midst of a three-week post-graduation adventure through India. I applied to the trip on a whim both because the topic intrigued me and because I was anxious to do more traveling. However, when I arrived in Germany, I found that the nation of Hitler guided me towards many answers in my quest to better understand my own Judaism.

Since my first trip to Israel in early 2007, I had become more aware of the size and shape of my individual identity. Specifically, I became aware of my own insecurities about being a Jew in a largely white, Christian world. At my affluent, homogenous private high school in Texas, my faith marked me as different. Certainly, when comparing my mess of dark, unruly curls with the blonde, orderly locks of my peers, it was easy to see we came from different stock. I was far from the only Jew in my grade. Several of us made the 20 to 30 minute drive each day from Houston's predominantly "Jewish" neighborhood into the WASPY neighborhood that housed my high school. Nevertheless, while I never admitted this feeling to myself, I always felt different. I carried this baggage with me to college and continued to struggle, albeit subconsciously, with being Jewish and "white" in a predominately white, Christian world. It wasn't until I arrived in Israel three years later that I finally felt at home. After a short and fast ten days of Birthright, I returned to the United States more confused than before. My liberal, social-activist self had always struggled with identifying as "Zionist," yet I unequivocally loved the existence and manifestation of the Jewish state. I decided to return to Israel to try to sort out my conflicted emotions, emotions that a friend had once classified as "cognitive dissonance."

Fast-forward to the end of my Germany Close Up experience and my arrival in Eretz Yisrael. When I landed in Israel before I started my *ulpan*,[5] I already knew that I wanted to return to a more traditional observance of Judaism. I had finally started to answer some questions about how I wanted to be Jewish. For me, marrying a Jew, surrounding myself with other Jewish people wasn't enough. I wanted to continue to be a part of the diverse social circles of which I had been a member in both high school and college. After choosing my roommates for Junior year, I had no compunction answering my mom that no, none of them were Jewish. However, I also knew that I needed Judaism to be a big part of my life.

Here is where my lesson from Germany came into play. Jews are a nation of survivors. We are a nation who endures. Despite all obstacles, we have survived these past 3000 years. Nevertheless, the slow creep of assimilation is succeeding where all of our external assailers have failed. Generation after generation more young Jews start the slow slide into the mainstream. Inch by inch they cast off their Jewish identity in favor of a more stylish, less different pass card into normalcy. As a kid, I always wanted to know more about my Judaism. I hated my ignorance about so much of my faith, and yet, I was considered one of the "Jewish" ones. I ran services and religious programming for my high school youth group. My most common request: make services as short and as painless as possible. I wanted to reintroduce a spark or connection to traditional Jewish practices.

My time in Germany inspired me to make good on this promise to myself. In college, I had already transitioned from an occasional participant in Shabbat services to one of the service's co-leaders. I wanted to push myself further. In the wake of my visit to Germany, I have become a much more observant Jew. No, I have not abandoned either my Feminist ideals or my sleeveless

5 *An intensive Hebrew program that often combines work and study.*

dresses, but nevertheless, I am choosing to guard the Shabbat and keep it holy. I turn off my cell phone; I walk away from my computer; I set aside two to three hours to prepare a Shabbat meal; I decline invitations from my friends to go out. I take at least twenty-four hours each week to celebrate my Judaism. Just as the Jews of Germany both today and in the past have molded Judaism to fit their modern selves, I too am struggling to create my own version of our faith.

The People of Israel's willingness to accept and welcome change is the key to our survival. With one eye to tradition and one eye to the future, we constantly reevaluate and morph in response to the needs of our communities. No community better embodies this spirit of adjustment than the Jews of Germany.

Perhaps nothing better illustrates our ability to change than the words of my grandfather, a Polish Jew born in the United States. After a six-month stay in Israel that included experiencing the entirety of "Operation Cast Lead," I returned to Germany for a brief visit before returning to the United States. When my grandfather heard the news, he exclaimed, "Thank G-d, she's back in Germany and out of Israel!"

Pride in Irony

Daniella Bondar

Standing in the middle of the House of the Wannsee Conference I look out the window. The world outside seems so bright, while all the light has been drained from where I stand. Careful not to touch anything, I walk around the table that stands sturdy in the middle of the room. I walk around and around expecting a different outcome each time. I am expecting the nausea to fade and let me move on to the rest of the house. I notice a paper hanging on the wall, the number of Jews left in each city. This place was supposed to decide the Jewish fate. This place held, most likely, the highest concentration of evil. The plans made in this place were supposed to annihilate us all. Suddenly the nausea is gone. I am still disgusted but I am not sad. I am proud. I have felt this before. I am standing in the very spot where it was decided that I should never be born. The irony in that is a simple pleasure.

This feeling was a pattern.

With each passing day the feeling of walking through history hit closer and closer. We spent ten days tracing steps and forming new ones. The first time I experienced this proud feeling was in the Sachsenhausen Concentration Camp. Walking through the empty camp I was disturbed but not angry like I thought I'd be. I was proud. I was the outcome of survivors, Jews who fought hard to make it through camps like Sachsenhausen. I was a part of something so strong it was able to knock down those who tried to break it.

All I knew of Germany, before my trip, was what it represented to me: the Nazi regime, in all its evil, trying to wipe the Jews off the face of the earth. Ever since I was little, my grandparents, Holocaust survivors, made it a point to tell me what had happened to them. To tell me how their parents and siblings were so brutally killed. They were teaching me history. Teaching me that the worst thing would be to let these stories go, to let people forget. You can't make stories like this up and you can't ever let them go. My mother told me that my grandma used to wake up in the middle of the night screaming and the whole house knew why.

The thing about growing up on the tragic tales of the Holocaust is that you can never get rid of them.

When I stepped out of the airport in Berlin, half of me wanted to turn around and go home. What was I doing there? What was the point? I thought that it was the dumbest choice I ever made. There was nothing I could learn that would change anything. I had been living my life with this feeling inside me that would never go away. I would always hate Germany, the people who lived there, and that was that. Why should I waste my time in a country that tried so hard to get rid of all my ancestors?

I looked through the museums and I watched the people on the street. I walked with my group and pretended I was somewhere else. I was seeing the old Germany, not the present one.

For me, Germany was somewhere I was never supposed to go. A forbidden place that held too many horrid memories. The city was like any other: hustle and bustle, people, stores, coffee, crowds. It was vibrant and cultured and there were so many things to look at, but none of it fazed me. The only thing I noticed was that the city was somehow different and that a group of young Jewish people was walking through it. Proudly.

Sitting in the synagogue on Friday night me, my group, and the congregants sang Hebrew songs at the top of our lungs. Right there outside for the whole world to hear. At that moment it was bigger than me. We all carried that proud feeling on our shoulders.

The uneasiness of being in Germany disappeared once I realized what it meant. I was a product of a demon's failure. I was a 19-year-old Jewish girl with 17 others walking through the streets of Germany. Laughing, eating, learning, having a good time. I would never have come to this inner peace if it wasn't for taking the trip.

Being in Germany gave me a new outlook on it all; my purpose became to show the world that we are still here. I wore my Jewish Star proudly around my neck, the entire trip. Every place I went I made sure to step very carefully. To leave a footprint, even if I was the only one who knew it was there. Everything I touched and every place I walked had a ghost. A mother, child, father, brother, son, daughter killed by the Nazis. Hitler did not want me to be there but I was. That's something no one can take away from me.

To be able to sit in a restaurant in Germany and look around and see all different types of people was a spectacular feeling. I am sure that I was not the only one who was proud to be in that spot at that very moment. I sat back sipping some water and gazed on in amazement. I had never thought about Germany being diverse. I had never thought about it running like any other place on earth.

I learned what Germany is doing to right its wrongs. I saw the new face and replaced my old images and notions with new ones. I saw new, friendly, likable people and made new connections. I understand how Germany has changed and how it will continue to do so. But when I think about my experience, when I think about my own personal Germany, the most present thought is the one of pride. The experience most important to me is that proud feeling I got. No other place in the world could have given me that. No other place could have made me understand what it actually means for me to be on this earth and part of the Jewish community. I have learned to understand things I never thought possible. It changed me.

I hate Hitler. And I hate the Nazis. And I hate what happened to my family. But I have turned the anger inside me into something else. I am proud that my grandparents and others like them were strong enough to pull through just to be able to stand proud knowing they, and they alone, are responsible for carrying on the Jewish nation.

The Nazis may have torn families apart, killed innocent people, and striven to achieve an ethnic cleansing, but they failed and that is what Germany is to me. Germany is a reminder of a great failure. The epicenter of evil has now become the emblem of pride.

The author in the Holocaust Tower at the Jewish Museum Berlin

Summer in Berlin

Graffiti in Berlin

Crossing Friedrichstraße

Louis Mittel

As I stir the milk and honey around in my cup, I wonder if I may be reading into all of this too much – all cafés serve milk and honey, not just Israeli ones. Still, I feel there is something special about Aroma Café. There is something that makes it more than just another place to grab a coffee in Berlin. As I struggle to put my finger on it, I reexamine the last few hours.

The skies are as grey as the smooth slab benches we sit on in the courtyard. Berlin's latest Holocaust museum, The Topography of Terror, has a modern facade, also grey. By this point in the trip, the pattern has become predictable: grey is the official color of Holocaust museums. But among the grey museums visited so far, this one stands out the most. The museum powerfully portrays the terror of the SS and Gestapo almost exclusively through photographs, with a collection that extends way beyond the famous ones that have become emblematic of the Holocaust (like the one of the young Jewish boy with the star on his jacket holding up his hands). Many images are new to me. There is one of SS officers cruelly taunting and assaulting Orthodox Jews in the streets that is particularly haunting.

By now the three of us have developed a post-museum routine. Mathan, Mardy, and I have been exploring Berlin for the past six days, and perhaps because of the nature of the trip, we have developed a comfort in our friendship unusual for people who didn't know each other just a week before. We meet outside and exchange our immediate reactions. At times our conversation is lighthearted and we crack jokes; other times it springboards into debates about history or philosophy.

But at today's gathering, there is unanimous agreement that the museum was very moving. Following a week of being inundated with Holocaust related content, none of us expected this museum to have such a significant impact on us. We talk a bit more, but we are mentally drained. It's our second museum of the day and our minds are saturated from staring at hundreds of disturbing photographs in the span of an hour. We also realize we are hungry. We decide to go to get something to eat.

As we leave the courtyard, we walk beside what looks like an archeological dig. A plaque explains that it is the partial excavation of underground SS offices. The museum is located at the site of the former SS Headquarters, a building that was bombed and destroyed during World War II. Looking at these underground ruins, one is drawn into a false sense that they represent history from an ancient time. They actually remind me of excavations I've seen in the Old City of Jerusalem on the way to the Western Wall from the Zion gate.

We cross a busy street and look out for an attractive restaurant. Beckoning to us is a place called Aroma Espresso Bar, sitting brightly on an adjacent corner. From a distance we can see that it is crowded (a good sign for foreigners deciding on a place to eat). I've heard positive reviews of Aroma from friends who have lived in Israel, I tell the group. Aroma is like the Israeli version of Starbucks, but better, and with more food offerings. It's an ubiquitous part of Israeli café culture. I didn't expect to come across it in Berlin, but I knew they had opened a branch in New York City, and Berlin's supposed to be the New York of Europe. In we go.

Through the glass doors we are met with a sleek and hip décor – flat screen TVs above the register illuminate the menu – and the pulsating rhythm of busy cappuccino machine steamers. The noise of a bustling café during lunch hour is refreshing after the somber but eerie quiet of the museum's visitors, all wandering the open hall in silence. The day's sights and sounds change fast!

Aroma Espresso Bar has a comprehensive coffee beverage menu, of course. It also serves fresh sandwiches and large bowls of vibrant salads with an Israeli flair. They have combo deals that give you a drink and a little taste of everything, served on a tray that looks like it could be from the McDonald's of the future. As a signature Aroma touch, each tray comes with one or two delicious Israeli milk chocolates.

We choose our meals, get our trays, and sit outside facing the museum at the SS site down the street. We dig into our sandwiches, sip our warm beverages, and continue our discussion. Mardy tells us about his grandfather from Poland who survived Auschwitz.

At some point I become acutely aware of the juxtaposition of the modern Israeli Aroma Espresso Bar, an expanding multinational restaurant chain, and the decaying SS Headquarters, a relic of German antisemitism, oppression, and crimes against humanity. It is a contrast that has stuck with me ever since.

Many people discuss the irony of German Jews buying a Mercedes-Benz. What about the irony of three American Jews, all grandsons of Holocaust survivors, sipping cappuccinos at an Israeli coffee shop across the street from the former SS and Gestapo Headquarters? The irony here is buried under the surface – quite literally in the case of the underground ruins.

To the Berliners who fill every seat and stool around me, Aroma is just an innocuously cool café; one like many others in any metropolis vying for the attention of the afternoon coffee drinker. Its Israeli identity is anonymous. Like the Jewish identities of the three of us; like my German last name – Mittel – and my corresponding German ancestry, unknown to the crowd of strangers. (Our American tourist identity, however, isn't as anonymous; anyone could gather that by sizing us up for a few seconds.) For me, however, these identities are buzzing, unwilling to be ignored. I am a Jew at an Israeli café in Germany.

How fast the trajectory of history can change! The Nazi plan once seemed a *fait accompli*, yet absolutely backfired. Not only did Nazi Germany collapse, the site of the headquarters of the SS and Gestapo, the core of Nazism and German ultra-nationalism, has been flipped by Germany into a permanent display of their incomprehensible terror. From Nazi pride to German shock and shame. Add to this, three Jewish young adults, children of German Jews, back in Germany on a trip paid for by Germany no less, with the intent of exposing us to places like this, to appreciate the Nazis' demise and see what achievements Germany has made since. Could the Nazis have ever possibly envisioned this conclusion?

Perhaps some imaginative Nazi officer who had a suspicion that Hitler's egomaniacal dream would drive Germany off a cliff could have almost imagined it. But Aroma Café, no way!

The Aroma Café is not just the Aroma Café: it represents a vibrant and happening Jewish state the Nazis never could have imagined. And ultimately, Hitler and the Nazis were in some way responsible for the metamorphosis of European Jewry into Israel. While Zionism as an idea and a movement existed before Nazism, it was the Holocaust that provided the impetus for its creation. This state goes on to flourish into the 21st century (with over 120 Aroma Cafés in Israel, locations in 7 other countries, and counting) and decides to drop one, as if in symbolic gesture as tribute to its roots, right next to the heart of the institution – and in the very heart of the country – that tried to annihilate its people.

Aroma also embodies a peculiar phenomenon that is the popularity of Germany – Berlin especially – for Israelis, a trend, which is somehow both understandable and bizarre. This was evident on our trip, as we encountered Israelis multiple times. We heard Hebrew spoken on the streets of Kreuzberg. One of our German tour guides was dating an Israeli. As part of the trip, we visited Kol Berlin, a startup Israeli radio station in Berlin. The head of the station explained briefly why there are so many Israelis in Berlin: Israel is a short plane ride away. Israel is a tiny country – its people feel a need to get out. Tel Aviv and Berlin share a similar liberalism and vivacity. Many Israelis have grandparents who came from Germany and therefore they have a natural curiosity about their past. Presented this way, Berlin is simply an attractive choice.

This account, of course, glosses over some details. It's not just that many Israelis have grandparents who came from Germany — many have grandparents who came from Auschwitz. The attitude of Israelis flocking to Berlin, while reasonable, is a complex dynamic that can at times seem cavalier. They claim to be conscious of how they relate to where they reside and that they have just developed ways to cope with the inherent strangeness. One method in particular, a timeless but provocative classic that my friends on the trip and I occasionally used as well, is comedy. We learn at Kol Berlin that the DJ incorporates Holocaust humor (in both Hebrew and German) throughout his program. These same airwaves in Berlin carried Hitler's tyrannical rants just over half a century ago. How could it get more ironic?

I can't help but connect this to something we were told by a speaker one day at the beginning of our trip. We all know that the slogan of Holocaust remembrance is "Never Again." But for the two parties, Germans and Jews, there are two sides to this proverbial proverb: Never Again Be Victims and Never Again Be Perpetrators. Back at Aroma, in front of me at our table, on opposite sides of Friedrichstraße we see manifestations of these Never Again components. We have, on one side, a museum devoted to locking the perpetration of the Holocaust into collective memory. On the other side, an entrepreneurial outpost represents a sample of the culture of a country, which was founded in part on the basis of the "Never Again Be Victims" principle.

The existence of an Israeli restaurant chain in Berlin across the street from the old offices of the SS is a testament to the revolution that both the Jewish and the German people have undergone since the time the SS building was standing and in full operation. Both people have rebounded, rebuilt, and reconfigured. The sides of the street have evolved. Where the SS Headquarters and perhaps a closed or vandalized Jewish bakery once stood now firmly reside the Topography of Terror Museum and the Aroma Espresso Bar. I wonder if we appreciate on both sides the degree of overhaul that the two replacements epitomize. In fact, it's the Topography of Terror exhibit that's loud; the Aroma Espresso Bar is silent.

The author

About the Authors

Rabbi Daniel Bogard, originally from St. Louis, Missouri, is the son of Robert and Denise Bogard. He currently lives in Peoria, Illinois, where he serves as co-rabbi of the Congregation Anshai Emeth along with his wife Rabbi Karen Bogard. In addition, Daniel is the Director of Bradley University Hillel, and lectures as an adjunct professor of Religious Studies at Bradley University. More importantly, Daniel is the father of Gavi Bogard, his beloved son! Daniel looks forward to his next opportunity to travel to Germany.

Daniel participated in the Germany Close Up trip run in affiliation with Hebrew Union College in May, 2010. His essay "Immersion in Living Waters: An American Rabbi's Journey through Modern Germany" was awarded third place in the 2011 Germany Close Up alumni essay competition.

Daniella Bondar is finishing up her college career with a degree in language and literature. She hopes to make it as a writer. In the meantime though, she plans to go on to grad school and hopefully earn a position in the publishing world. Till then you can find her enjoying life in NYC, surrounded by books, records, pens, and paper.

Daniella participated in the Germany Close Up trip for students run in affiliation with Hillel in July, 2010.

Kerry Chaplin is studying to be a rabbi at the Ziegler School of Rabbinic Studies. She has worked and volunteered as a community organizer for over 15 years. In addition to her studies, she teaches religious school, and is a leader in a variety of multi-faith economic and social justice campaigns. Kerry holds both a B.A. in Religious Studies and an M.A. in Non-Profit Management from Washington University in St. Louis. She lives in Los Angeles with her wife Julia, and plays wing for her Santa Monica Women's Rugby Club.

Kerry participated in the Germany Close Up trip for students run in affiliation with the Jewish Theological Seminary and the American Jewish University in January, 2011. Her essay "Knowing Ollie" was awarded second place in the 2011 Germany Close Up alumni essay competition.

Hadas Cohen is an Israeli lawyer. She moved to New York to pursue a Master's degree at Columbia University, and is currently completing a Ph.D. in Political Science at the New School University. Hadas has worked in Ghana and

Venezuela on human rights and education related projects and has written extensively about the Israeli-Palestinian conflict, Israeli society, and about the relationship between the memory of the Holocaust and Israeli nationalism.

Hadas participated in the Germany Close Up trip for young professionals run in affiliation with the Jewish Community Center of Manhattan in October-November, 2008. Her essay "The Impossibilities of Transcendence – or why I felt bad because my Grandparents did not have to survive Auschwitz" was awarded first place in the 2009 Germany Close Up alumni essay competition.

Liz Foreman works professionally as an Assistant Regional Director in the New York Regional Office of the Anti-Defamation League, where she coordinates outreach to the law enforcement community, campus affairs, and international relations. She is currently a Master's Candidate in Public Administration at Baruch College, City University of New York, and holds a Bachelor of Arts from Rutgers University, Phi Beta Kappa, in Jewish Studies and Political Science. Liz is an avid genealogist, who has traced her family's history five generations in the United States; and also enjoys making jewelry, watching the Yankees, and practicing yoga.

Liz participated in the Germany Close Up trip for young professionals run in July-August, 2008. Her essay "Honoring the Memory of the Past" was awarded third place in the 2009 Germany Close Up alumni essay competition.

Ira Glasser completed his Master's Degree in Adolescent Education in Social Studies at City University of New York – Hunter College. He is currently the History Department Coordinator, plans and leads the eighth grade Israel trip, and teaches seventh and eighth grade history at the Rodeph Sholom School, a Reform Jewish Day School in Manahattan, New York.

Ira participated in the Germany Close Up trip for young teachers run in affiliation with the Holocaust Centre of Toronto in July, 2009.

Simon Goldberg is the Jewish Studies Coordinator at Elsa High School in Hong Kong. Born in London, he grew up in Jerusalem and moved to New York in 2003, where he obtained a Bachelor's degree in History from Yeshiva University. Simon has spent over half a decade working in the field of genocide education and activism. In addition to teaching, he serves as the Executive Director of Triangles of Truth, an international movement of students who honor and remember Holocaust victims by working to end present-day genocide.

Simon participated in the Germany Close Up trip for students run in affiliation with Yeshiva University in June, 2010.

Mary Rachel Gould is an assistant professor of communication at Saint Louis University. Her research interests include the study of transgression and discipline in contemporary culture with a particular emphasis on the prison system, dark tourism, and popular culture.

Mary participated in the Germany Close Up trip for students run in affiliation with Brandeis University in December, 2008. Her essay "Making History Public: Germany's Efforts to Remember its Past," which she co-authored with fellow alumni Rachel E. Silverman, was awarded second place in the 2009 Germany Close Up alumni essay competition.

Adam Heltzer is the Director of Agriculture and Food Security at the Louis Berger Group in Washington, D.C. Son to a formerly Orthodox mother and a Reform father, Adam was raised Conservative and has always enjoyed contemplating contemporary Jewish identity. Following a March of the Living Birthright trip in 2004 he began an in-depth research project into his family history, locating the ship manifests of each of his immigrant ancestors. He was grateful for the opportunity to continue his exploration of Jewish identity and experience through the Germany Close Up program. Adam has an MBA from the Harvard Business School and an MPA from the Harvard Kennedy School.

Adam participated in the Germany Close Up trip for young professionals run in December, 2008.

Marissa Kaplan grew up in New York, USA, and later moved to Israel where she lived for several years. She graduated from Tel Aviv University with a Master's in English Literature. Currently, she is living in Quito, Ecuador, teaching Hebrew and Jewish Studies.

Marissa participated in the Germany Close Up trip for students run in affiliation with the American Jewish Committee's ACCESS program in August, 2010.

Marc Elias Keller grew up in Bucks County, Pennsylvania, and earned degrees in Anthropology and Urban Studies from the University of Pennsylvania. He has been a freelance and journalistic writer in Philadelphia and San Diego, as well as publishing short fiction in various literary magazines. He lives in Philadelphia.

Marc participated in the Germany Close Up trip run in affiliation with the American Jewish Committee's ACCESS program in May, 2010.

Caroline Kessler received her Bachelor's degree in Creative Writing, with a minor in Religion, from Carnegie Mellon University in December, 2011. She has studied abroad in India, worked as the American Jewish Committee Goldman Fellow for the Warsaw-based nonprofit, The Forum for Dialogue Among Nations, and volunteered in Israel with the Jewish National Fund. A poet at heart, she's currently a candidate manager at a technical recruiting firm in San Francisco, where she bicycles, makes zines, and plans her next adventure.

Caroline participated in the Germany Close Up trip for students run in affiliation with the American Jewish Committee's ACCESS program in August, 2010.

Erin Levi holds a B.A. in French from Georgetown University (COL '05) and a Master of Letters in Middle East and Central Asian Security Studies from the University of St. Andrews in Scotland (MECASS '07) where she was a Ransome Scholar. After several stints abroad – internships and study programs in Italy, Uzbekistan, Vietnam, and Scotland – where she accumulated a myriad of languages along the way, Erin finally moved back stateside, taking a travel PR job at DQMPR in New York City, where she handles media relations and marketing for destinations, tour companies, airlines, and hotels. She still dreams of one day becoming a successful travel writer or diplomat, or even both!

Erin participated in the Germany Close Up trip for students run in affiliation with the American Jewish Committee's ACCESS program in August, 2010.

Rabbi Maura Linzer is from suburban Pittsburgh, Pennsylvania. She attended Washington University in St. Louis, where she graduated with honors, receiving a B.A. majoring in both Psychology and Jewish, Islamic, and Near Eastern Studies with a minor in Modern Hebrew. She began rabbinical school at Hebrew Union College – Jewish Institute of Religion (HUC-JIR) in the summer of 2006. She earned an M.A. in Hebrew Letters from HUC-JIR in 2009 and an M.A. in Middle East Studies at Ben Gurion University in the Negev in 2010. She was ordained from HUC-JIR in June, 2012 and her graduation thesis was entitled "The Holocaust and the Message of Hope in Rabbinic Homilies, 1933-1942." Maura is currently pursuing an M.A. in Religious Education from HUC-JIR. Maura is married to Liad Itzhaky, and they celebrated the birth of their daughter, Sarah Eve, in July, 2012.

Maura participated in the Germany Close Up trip for students run in affiliation with Hebrew Union College in May-June, 2009.

Louis Mittel grew up in Atlanta, Georgia, and received his undergraduate degree at Tufts University in Boston. He is currently studying in his second year of a Ph.D. program in Statistics at Columbia University in New York City.

Louis participated in the Germany Close Up trip for students run in affiliation with the American Jewish Committee's ACCESS program in August, 2010. His essay "Crossing Friedrichstraße" was awarded first place in the 2011 Germany Close Up alumni essay competition.

Rebecca Pedinoff finished college and found herself living for the past several years in beautiful Oakland, California. She visited Germany exactly 75 years after her grandparents left, to see if the stories were true. She liked what she saw and plans on returning soon, possibly for graduate school.

Rebecca participated in the Germany Close Up trip for young professionals run in February, 2010.

Yehuda Rothstein is a graduate of the University of Michigan, Ann Arbor, where he studied Middle-Eastern and North African Studies, Judaic Studies, and Afro and African-American studies. A graduate of Cornell Law School, and an Albert Heit Scholarship Recipient, he received a Juris Doctor and an LL.M in International & Comparative Law in 2010. After law school, he clerked for a Federal District Court judge in New York City and now works as an attorney at a New York City law firm.

Yehuda participated in the Germany Close Up trip for students run in affiliation with the American Jewish Committee's ACCESS program in August, 2010.

Eryn Schultz is a management consultant with Accenture. She graduated from Georgetown University where she studied International Politics and Economics and began attending Harvard Business School in the Fall of 2012. She loves to travel and has gone back to Germany twice since Germany Close Up ended.

Eryn participated in the Germany Close Up trip for young professionals run in July-August, 2008.

Rachel E. Silverman is an assistant professor of communication at Embry Riddle Aeronautical University. Her research interests focus on the intersection of Jewish and queer identities in popular culture, women's health, and social justice pedagogy.

Rachel participated in the Germany Close Up trip for students run in affiliation with Brandeis University in December, 2008. Her essay "Making History Public: Germany's Efforts to Remember its Past," which she co-authored with fellow alumni Mary Rachel Gould, was awarded second place in the 2009 Germany Close Up alumni essay competition.

About the Editors

Dr. Dagmar Pruin is the Executive Director of Aktion Sühnezeichen Friedensdienste e.V. (Action Reconciliation Service for Peace) and Director of Germany Close Up. She studied Theology and Jewish Studies at the University of Hamburg, the Hebrew University in Jerusalem, the University of Göttingen, and the Humboldt University of Berlin, from which she received her Ph.D. in 2003. Following her studies, she initially began a career in academia with a position at the Humboldt University, where she was also a founding member of the Program on Religion and Politics, and visiting fellowships in South Africa and the United States. In Fall 2007, she moved out of the academic field to realize the program Germany Close Up.

Dr. Hermann Simon was born in Berlin in 1949. He studied History and Oriental Studies at the Humboldt University, Berlin and Oriental numismatics in Prague, receiving his Ph.D. in 1976. From 1988 to 1995, he directed the reconstruction of the New Synagogue as the Centrum Judaicum. He has directed the New Synagogue since July, 1988. His publications include *Das Berliner Jüdische Museum in der Oranienburger Straße* and articles on numismatics and the history of Jews in Germany.

About Germany Close Up

Germany Close Up – American Jews Meet Modern Germany is a youth encounter program, which was established in October 2007. It is administered by the New Synagogue Berlin – Centrum Judaicum Foundation, a Berlin based Jewish organization, and was conceptualized by Dagmar Pruin. Germany Close Up is funded by a grant from the German Government's Transatlantic Program, which draws on funds from the European Recovery Program (ERP) of the German Federal Ministry of Economics and Technology. As such, the program aims to encourage German-Jewish-North American dialogue as well as to strengthen the involvement of the North American Jewish community in transatlantic relations. To achieve this aim, Germany Close Up brings groups of young, North American Jews to Germany for short educational trips lasting one to two weeks. These trips aim to give participants the opportunity to gain a firsthand experience of modern Germany. Participants are students and young professionals aged between 18 and 35.

Since its establishment, Germany Close Up has brought more than 1400 participants in almost 70 groups to Germany. The majority of Germany Close Up groups are organized together with Jewish partner organizations based in North America and which cover a diverse range of religious and political backgrounds. To date, these organizations have included universities (Hebrew Union College, the Jewish Theological Seminary, the American Jewish University, Yeshiva University, and Brandeis University), the American Jewish Committee, the Anti-Defamation League, Hillel, KIVUNIM, the Council of Jewish Emigré Community Organizations, Camp Ramah, the Rabbinical Assembly, Limmud, the Orthodox Union, Global Round Table, B'nai B'rith NYC, the Jewish Community Center of Manhattan, the Holocaust Centre of Toronto, Classrooms without Borders, and He'bro. Although the majority of Germany Close Up programs are run as cooperations with individual organizations, most programs are also open for individual application. In addition, Germany Close Up also runs some of its trips without an affiliated cooperation partner. These two measures combined aim to ensure that the program reaches out to both affiliated and unaffiliated North American Jews.

Each Germany Close Up program attempts to provide a framework for participants to experience and explore contemporary Germany. In so doing, it does not try to present one set picture, but rather to expose participants to a variety of elements that make up Germany today. All programs contain units looking at both the past and the present. Units focusing on the past explore

Germany's efforts to deal with the memory of the Shoah and the Nazi terror up to the present day. Units focusing on the present consider the changes in German politics and society over the past decades. Each program also looks at the reemergence of Jewish life in Germany and the current growth of the Jewish community.

During the program, participants are confronted with various questions relevant to understanding modern German society. These questions are presented both through meetings and discussions as well as excursions and other activities. All groups meet with a representative of the German Federal Foreign Office and a member of the German Federal Parliament. They also have meetings with representatives of grass roots movements and Jewish organizations, academics and journalists, members of the Jewish community, and young Germans their own age, both Jewish and non-Jewish. Germany Close Up student programs also often include a study day or session together with German students, during which both sides share their different perspectives on a single topic. The Germany Close Up experience is rounded out by visits to museums and memorials, and to a town or city outside Berlin. All trips include a visit to the Memorial to the Murdered Jews of Europe and to the Jewish Museum in Berlin. In addition, all groups visit a former concentration camp, such as Sachsenhausen or Buchenwald. Every group is taken on a walking tour of Berlin's former Jewish neighborhood, on which they often encounter "Stolpersteine" for the first time.

Beyond these common units, many Germany Close Up trips also have their own special focus. This special focus is often aligned with the goals and priorities of the affiliated partner organization. Each year, Germany Close Up runs a program with a focus on interreligious dialogue. Trips with a focus on Jewish history and the roots of the Ashkenazic community in Germany are also run regularly for rabbinical and cantorial students. Individual programs have also been run focusing on green energy and LGBT issues, respectively. Several trips have also been scheduled to allow participants to simultaneously take part in larger events concurrently taking place in Germany. Trips have been run that included participation in a Limmud conference, attendance at the Berlinale, Berlin's international film festival, and attendance at the decennial passion play in Oberammergau.

Germany Close Up participant and guide

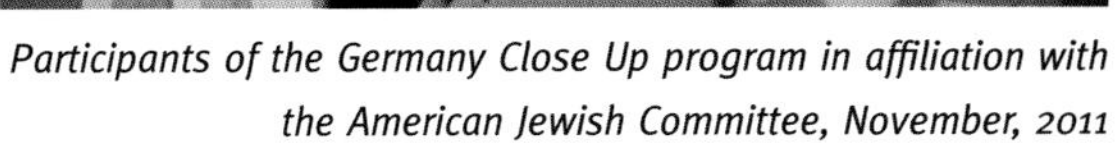

Participants of the Germany Close Up program in affiliation with the American Jewish Committee, November, 2011

Germany Close Up
American Jews Meet Modern Germany

Stiftung Neue Synagoge Berlin – Centrum Judaicum

Photo Acknowledgements

We would hereby like to acknowledge and thank the following people for providing us with the the photographs used in this volume:

p. 9 (top and bottom) Jessica Schilling
p. 11 © Stiftung Neue Synagoge Berlin – Centrum Judaicum; Photographer: Anna Fischer
p. 19 Hadas Cohen
p. 25 Mary Rachel Gould and Rachel E. Silverman
p. 27 Heidi Moore
p. 30 © Stiftung Neue Synagoge Berlin – Centrum Judaicum; Photographer: Anna Fischer
p. 34 Liz Foreman
p. 38 Simon Goldberg
p. 43 Kerry Chaplin
p. 49 Simon Goldberg
p. 54 Simon Goldberg
p. 60 Simon Goldberg
p. 65 Samuel Pollack
p. 71 Marla Kaplan
p. 80 © Passionsspiele Oberammergau 2010
p. 87 Adam Moscoe
p. 93 Adam Moscoe
p. 96 Jessica Schilling
p. 105 Daniella Bondar
p. 106 (top and bottom) Rachael Silverstein
p. 111 Mathan Glezer
p. 121 (top and bottom) Jessica Schilling

Front cover (top to bottom) Heidi Moore; © Stiftung Neue Synagoge Berlin – Centrum Judaicum; Photographer: Anna Fischer; Jessica Schilling

Back cover (top to bottom) Rachel Schwartz; Heidi Moore; Kerry Chaplin

Imprint

Inh. Dr. Nora Pester
Wilhelmstrasse 118, 10963 Berlin
info@hentrichhentrich.de
http://www.hentrichhentrich.de

Layout: Michaela Weber

1st edition November 2013

Printed in the E.U.
ISBN 978-3-95565-006-3

The program Germany Close Up – American Jews Meet Modern Germany is sponsored by the Federal Government of the Federal Republic of Germany using funds of the Federal Ministry of Economics and Technology in its function as the administrator of the ERP Fund.